OTHER BOOKS BY ROBERT BRUSTEIN

The Theatre of Revolt

Seasons of Discontent

The Third Theatre

Revolution as Theatre

The Culture Watch

EDITOR

Selected Plays and Prose of August Strindberg

CRITICAL MOMENTS

ROBERT BRUSTEIN

CRITICAL
MOMENTS

Reflection on
Theatre & Society
1973-1979

RANDOM HOUSE
NEW YORK

All rights reserved under International and Pan-American Copyright Conventions. Published in the United States by Random House, Inc., New York, and simultaneously in Canada by Random House of Canada Limited, Toronto.

"Styron's Choice" was first published in *Vogue*. All other selections have previously appeared in the following publications: the *Atlantic Monthly*, *Decade* magazine, the *New Republic*, the New York *Times*, and *yale/theatre*.

Grateful acknowledgment is made to the following for permission to reprint previously published material: Doubleday & Company, Inc.: "Vineyard Passage," copyright © 1980 by Robert Brustein, from the book *On the Vineyard* by Peter Simon. Reprinted by permission of Doubleday & Company, Inc. Farrar, Straus & Giroux, Inc.: Excerpts from *Ibsen: Letters and Speeches* by Evert Sprinchorn. Copyright © 1964 by Evert Sprinchorn. Reprinted by permission of Hill & Wang (a division of Farrar, Straus & Giroux, Inc.). The New York Times: "The Theatre Audience: A House Divided," "John Simon (Uneasy Stages and Singularities)," "Pauline Kael (Reeling)," "H. L. Mencken (The New Mencken Letters)," "Tennessee Williams (Letters to Donald Wyndham)," "Art Versus Advocacy," "The Future of the Endowments," "Broadway Anglophilia," "The Crack in the Chimney: Theatre in the Age of Einstein," "No Sound, No Fury" are reprinted from *The New York Times*. Copyright © 1975/76/77/78 by The New York Times Company. Reprinted by permission.

Library of Congress Cataloging in Publication Data
Brustein, Robert Sanford, 1927-
Critical moments.
1. Theater—United States—Addresses, essays, lectures. I. Title.
PN2266. B718   792'.0973   79-3804
ISBN 0-394-51093-3

Manufactured in the United States of America
98765432
First Edition

This book is dedicated
to the "family"— the American Repertory
Theatre Company — and to
its departed mother

Acknowledgments

A FEW of the many people to whom I am deeply obliged: Sy Peck and Bill Honan at the New York *Times;* Martin Peretz at the *New Republic;* Penny Pigott and Rob Orchard at the Rep; Jan and Jeremy Geidt; my students and former students at the Yale School of Drama . . . and, always, Norma.

ALSO the publishers, editors, and copy readers of the following magazines, in which these pieces have appeared: the New York *Times,* the *New Republic, Partisan Review, Decade, yale/theatre* and *Theatre, Atlantic Monthly,* and *Vogue.*

FINALLY, Robert Loomis and Robert Bernstein at Random House.

Contents

IV. Leisure Moments: *Satires, Stories, Plays*

V. Personal Moments: *Reflections and Responses*

Introduction

THE ESSAYS, reviews, speeches, interviews, stories, and plays collected in this book were all written between 1973 and 1979, which is probably the only unity I should legitimately claim for them. These years, however, were critical moments in the life of the nation, the performing arts, and the Yale institution with which I had been associated since 1966; I venture to say they were critical in my own life as well. For that reason, I would like to propose another unifying element for this book—a sense of crisis which, in my moments of criticism, I was trying to understand and announce.

The seventies—that whey-faced decade—is still being explored for an identifying characteristic that might add some color to its pale, cheesy features. The political silhouette of the period is just beginning to emerge: an epoch of fits and starts, of sudden spasms, of high expectations fizzling out to a chorus of raspberries. Richard Nixon, reelected to office with the highest plurality in American history, gets ensnared in Watergate and resigns in disgrace; Gerald Ford loses his own bid for the presidency after handing a blanket pardon to the very man who placed him in power; Jimmy Carter, an unknown from Georgia, smiles his way to a brilliant victory, then loses the confidence of the electorate through his political incompetence and incertitude.

These events reinforce a curious characteristic of our recent history—its abortive nature: Not since Dwight Eisenhower removed his golf clubs from the White House in 1960 has an American President been able either to win or to complete a second term. These two decades of politicus interruptus have turned us into a skeptical, bewildered, fragmented nation, with a deep suspicion of authority, and a nervous, itchy compulsion to trade in our leaders periodically with our automobiles and washing machines. As above, so below in this disposable society. Our distrust and uncertainty, leaching down from the political sphere, begins to enter every area of our experience, whether in the home or in industry, whether in the foundation world or academic life or the performing arts. The machinery of leadership gets clogged with rust, unhinges itself, drops its parts.

Compare these decades with any earlier period, and it becomes clear how we are beginning to lose some of our respect for stability and permanence. It is almost inconceivable today that Franklin Roosevelt was once elected to a fourth term, or that executives usually remained in office until they were visited by death, disease, or disgrace (sometimes even then they stayed—Mayor Curley of Boston was reelected for another term while sitting in jail). Today, it's difficult to remember just who is in charge of what. It's not that our leaders are unfamiliar to us; quite the opposite, the media introduce us to every secret of their private lives. But the very mechanism that makes these leaders instantly known makes them vulnerable to instant replacement.

Consider, if you will, this incomplete list of recent leadership changes in the performing arts alone:

- Livingston Biddle replaces Nancy Hanks as chairman of the National Endowment for the Arts.
- Joseph Duffey replaces Ronald Berman as chairman of the National Endowment for the Humanities.
- Franklin Thomas replaces McGeorge Bundy as director of the Ford Foundation.
- Walter Kerr replaces Richard Eder as theatre critic for the New York *Times,* just two years after Eder replaced Clive Barnes.
- Beverly Sills replaces Julius Rudel as director of the City Center Opera Company.
- Mikhail Baryshnikov replaces Lucia Chase as director of the American Ballet Theatre.

- Joseph Papp relinquishes control of the Vivian Beaumont Theatre at Lincoln Center and, after a two-year interregnum, is replaced by Richmond Crinkley, who announces a six-person directorate.
- Martin Feinstein resigns as executive director of the Kennedy Center under pressure from the board.
- Frank Dunlop is dropped as director of the resident theatre company at the Brooklyn Academy of Music and is replaced by David Jones.
- Alvin Epstein is fired from the Guthrie Theatre in Minneapolis, only one full season after he replaced Michael Langham as artistic director.
- Alan Schneider is dropped after two years as head of the Drama Division of Juilliard and is replaced by Michael Langham.
- Lloyd Richards replaces Robert Brustein as dean of the Yale School of Drama and director of the Yale Repertory Theatre.

The last item concedes my personal involvement in the events being observed, and the reader is perfectly welcome to dismiss my analysis as a form of special pleading. I do not claim to be a disinterested observer of this historical process, and thus I may very well be disqualified from discussing it at all. Still, I don't believe that my particular case is typical of what I'm trying to describe. For one thing, I held my post for thirteen years, so I can hardly complain of having been abruptly flicked aside before getting a chance to prove my programs, and I can't ascribe my departure from Yale to America's fickleness toward leaders. I have mentioned myself, in short, for the sake of inclusiveness, believing it more honest to state my involvement than to ignore it, despite atypical circumstances.

Another warning about my generalizations. Since each of the changes mentioned above is the result of an extremely complicated set of causes, no single reason can accurately be assigned to all. Nevertheless, even this incomplete list of dismissals, resignations, withdrawals, and replacements—coming along in such a brief period of time—is enough to suggest that something tumultuous was happening in the performing arts world over the last few years. If this tumult does not share a common cause, I believe it to describe a similar pattern.

To define this pattern has been the motive impulse behind much of my recent writing, where I have tried to chronicle these convulsions, to speculate about their several causes, and, if possible, to try to forestall them. It is for this reason that a whole section of my book is taken up with funding; the prime and crucial basis for these transactions I believe to be economic. It was during these years that subsidy for the arts from outside agencies was being whittled away, and there was subsequent pressure, both internally and externally, to make them more responsive to popular taste. Many of the performing arts institutions founded in the sixties were rockets sent up by the "cultural explosion"—that being the popular code phrase for a sense that the United States was lagging, by comparison with other civilized countries, in support for the arts. The new national interest in subsidizing performance was probably excited by the same competitive impulse that increased arms production, after a "missile gap" was discovered, and that improved federal support for education after the Russians beat us into space with Sputnik. In those affluent times, the United States was rich enough and confident enough to accommodate military, social, educational, and cultural spending, within the same federal budget.

As soon as the economy began to fall apart, however, the experiment in patronage for the performing arts began to splinter too. First the private foundations withdrew their backing and turned their attention to urban problems; then the federal and state foundations, expected to take up the slack, failed to compensate with sufficient funds. Worse, these government agencies were becoming seriously politicized by lob-

bies, legislators, and a populist administration. When unem-
ployment increased, accompanied by a fearful rise in the inflation rate, aid to culture was perceived, in many government
circles, as a frivolity draining more essential social programs.
The straightforward procedure would have been to transfer
the resources of the National Endowments to the Department
of Health, Education, and Welfare; this, at least, would have
spared us the official hypocrisy. Instead, the performing arts
institutions were subtly pressured to demonstrate their social
usefulness in order to justify their grants; no longer was artistic quality the primary criterion of value.

The phony debate between "elitism and populism" was simply the subterfuge through which the arts were asked to conform to social-utilitarian pressures. Afraid of being accused of
snobbism, exclusiveness, aloofness, or some other horrible
aristocratic failing, the performing arts institutions were soon
engaged in the debilitating charade of proving their importance to a democratic society—whether through artists-in-
schools programs or touring disadvantaged areas or advancing ethnic and racial identity claims or forming mobile units;
in short, any form of social uplift for which there might be
federal money available. Their prime responsibility now was
not to the creative imagination but rather to devising a convincing demonstration that they had a useful purpose to the
body politic. Instead of developing artists and artworks, they
were asked to concentrate their energies on dissemination.

Engaged in a mad scramble for the same limited funds, these
institutions had the unpleasant alternative of becoming as
competitive toward each other as soap and detergent companies, or herding together in a huge lobbying venture to put
pressure on politicians for more arts appropriations. Prodded
by service organizations—those proliferating arts bureaucra-
cies spawned by the complications of government guidelines
and regulations—performing groups were encouraged to
bureaucratize themselves as well, forming a consortium that
would soon include not only dance and opera companies,

theatres and orchestras, but also hospitals, museums, cancer funds, and other charities. Informed that everything "non-profit" had similar interests, they were asked to enter the political system even if this cost them their artistic identity.

Arts advocacy was only one of the stratagems for ensuring the survival of the performing arts. Another was providing more popular and accessible programing. Still another was persuading such star performers to function as artistic directors of companies as Beverly Sills and Baryshnikov—chosen, no doubt, for their redoubtable creative vision, but perhaps also because their lustrous names would more readily attract audiences and backers. Still another method of shoring up these companies was the alliance—particularly prevalent in the theatre—between nonprofit groups and commercial interests. The resident theatres began to act as one of the chief suppliers of dramatic product to Broadway, whether functioning as tryout houses for packaged material or originating their own productions—practical methods of ensuring a flow of royalties into their shrinking coffers.

But however profitable this new affiliation may have been, it signaled the end of an era when the resident theatre movement could proudly consider itself an artistic alternative to Broadway; and I found myself in the embarrassing position of urging my gifted students toward these theatres at the very moment when some of them were losing their moral and creative force. Perhaps I should have known that our system doomed this experiment from the start. The private artist is rarely prevented from creating by economic constraints. T. S. Eliot could write his poetry while working as a bank teller; Wallace Stevens could support his literary ambitions with his insurance firm; William Carlos Williams could practice verse and medicine in the same week. But a dance company can't work in a bank, a theatre company can't sell insurance, an opera company can't heal the sick. Lacking generous subsidy, the performing arts become subject to the vagaries of the economic system, and this means an inevitable impairment in ambition and quality.

For there are only three ways for the performing arts to survive—either through the box office or through patronage or, most desirably, through a combination of the two. When patronage disappears, the law of the box office demands that risk, adventure, and creative aspiration disappear as well. The pressure on companies to be "more responsive to the community" is simply another form of box-office rhetoric, regardless of how many brownie points it earns in Washington. And rather than leading the public through a process devoted to expanding its vision, the performing arts institution becomes just another mirror of public taste. The changes in leadership that have recently been transforming the performing arts may be an effort to relate them more closely to the common will.

Matthew Arnold wrote in *Culture and Anarchy:* "Plenty of people will try to give the masses, as they call them, an intellectual food prepared and adapted in the way they think proper for the actual condition of the masses. Culture works differently. It does not try to reach down . . . it seeks to do away with classes. This is the social idea. The men of culture are the true apostles of equality. The great men of culture are those who have a passion for diffusing, for making prevail, for carrying from one end of society to the other the best knowledge, the best ideas of their time. . . ." This dream of cultural classlessness, of disseminating not just art and thought but the *best* art and thought, is now being replaced by another impulse, to adapt to the untutored demands of the masses in the name of democratic ideals. This "revolution against taste," as Edmund Gosse called it, does not threaten our private thinkers and artists, who will somehow still manage to function, so much as the collective existence of our serious public arts.

Sounds dismal, no? But there is always a glimpse of green on the barren landscape, if only because Americans are too restless to remain content for long with a single cultural pattern. Another swing of the historical pendulum—another political jolt to make us fear we are falling behind the Russians or the English or the Swiss or the Laplanders—and once again the machinery for supporting the arts may get lubricated. This country embraces so many tastes and expectations, so many diverse demands, that it will not hold still long enough to be catalogued or photographed. Our fragmented culture can be a source of hope as well as despair; our fickle desire for change can also produce surprise. Perhaps the next round of critical moments will blossom into golden creative hours and days.

A NOTE ON ORGANIZATION. This book is divided into five sections or "moments." 1) *Polemical Moments,* in which are discussed certain critics and contemporaries, along with the current state of theatre criticism; 2) *Fiscal Moments,* in which the main topic is funding for the arts; 3) *Cultural Moments,* in which are treated the larger issues of art and society, with particular attention to the relationship between high and popular culture; 4) *Leisure Moments,* in which certain social-cultural concerns are satirized in a lighter vein; and 5) *Personal Moments,* where the past is memorialized and the future embraced. I beg the reader's pardon for the valedictory note that concludes the book. It is the only way I know to convey the kind of beginnings and endings in which I am now engaged.

PART I

POLEMICAL MOMENTS:
Critics and Contemporaries

CONTENTS

ONE

Where Are the Repertory Critics?

THERE HAS BEEN so much concern in recent years over the languishing health of the American theatre that it may have escaped notice how the diagnosticians are ailing too—and may even be helping to infect the patient. I refer, of course, to the drama critics, reviewers, and commentators, that breed of hardworking, long-suffering journalists who have been charged with the task of looking upon the incredible disarray of our theatre and saying something coherent about it. What is the condition of present-day American drama criticism? Is this profession acting as an aid or an obstacle to the development of a viable American theatre? What should be the function of the play reviewer—whether he writes daily, weekly, monthly, or irregularly—in relation to the dramatic works he scrutinizes?

My own views on these questions have been influenced by the fact that I work in a dual capacity in the theatre, both as a critic and as artistic director of a company, so you are perfectly free to discount what I say as either the prejudice of a

critical practitioner or the defensiveness of a theatre professional who is subject to criticism himself. But I hope I have
been able to muster enough detachment about the critical
process, through my association with it on both sides of the
footlights, to support my contention that theatre criticism in
this country is in a deplorable state, partly because it has failed
to keep pace with the institutional and aesthetic changes that
have been occurring on the American stage.

I had some insight into the roots of this problem during a
recent FACT Conference on the American theatre at Princeton where, during a panel on criticism on which I served, it was
immediately clear that no intelligent discussion of the subject
was possible, given the differing interests of the groups involved. The representatives of the commercial theatre per-
sisted in their belief that the function of criticism was to provide as much space as possible in the print and broadcast
media for helping to sell their shows. The representatives of
the resident theatres, though also grateful for good reviews
and decent coverage, seemed equally interested in the reflective and analytical aspect of the critical process.

In other words, play reviewing was being evaluated on the
one hand by those who looked upon it as a medium of publicity
exclusively, and on the other, by those who considered it primarily a medium of thought, and while both sides had reason
to complain about the current situation, it struck me that most
drama criticism at the present time was designed to satisfy only
the first group. It is not hard to understand why. The reduc-
tion in the number of New York newspapers has decimated the
ranks of theatre reviewers, with the result that success or failure on the New York stage now rests, for all intents and purposes, with a handful of men, if it is not entirely in the lap of
the daily reviewers for the New York *Times*. Burdened with
responsibility for nothing less than the survival of the commercial theatre, such men are under increasing pressure to work
up interest in Broadway shows, so it is no wonder that some
of them have begun to write like press agents, using a vocabu-

lary more appropriate to advertising than to criticism. The superlatives one always finds quoted in theatre ads—"Miss this performance at your peril!" . . . "I've never seen a funnier show!" . . . "Best Musical of the Season!"—have become more frequent and hyperbolic over recent years because reviewers are now painfully aware that every time they tap their typewriters, they are also ringing the bells of the theatre's cash registers. (And not only the cash registers . . . Even foundation grants and subscription lists can be affected by New York reviews, which is why nonprofit theatres, though less dependent on the box office than Broadway, will also cite these notices in their brochures—usually quoting the accolade most of them have received from Clive Barnes as "One of the best resident theatres in the country!")

I suppose this kind of development is inevitable in a system where audiences lack the theatregoing instinct, not to mention confidence in their own taste, and therefore have to be stimulated by a reviewer's prose before they will buy a ticket. The trouble is that much of this critical enthusiasm is so obviously trumped-up that it runs the risk of achieving the opposite effect than that intended. Promiscuous praise not only corrupts the language, it eventually shakes the trust of the reader in the writer's credibility, since inflated criticism is like an inflated economy—it can quickly debase the currency. Proclaiming the arrival of false masterpieces too often in a season is almost as pernicious as ignoring those rare works that have some genuine merit: It creates a condition, as Lionel Trilling has put it, where "a lie is established in society"—and our society is already groaning under its burden of mendacity. Finally it deludes the public into believing that a reviewer's opinion about a play or a production is of profound significance, that judgments of value are the most important element of the critic's craft.

As a matter of fact, even the opinions of the most discerning critics are the least enduring part of their writing, and that is why some fine reviews (say, Bernard Shaw's notice of *The Im-*

portance of Being Earnest) have survived when the critic has utterly misjudged the worth of the play. Speaking as one who is hardly shy about expressing opinions, I have never been able to frame an adequate reply to those who ask why my reviews should be taken any more seriously than theirs, primarily because I'm always conscious of how much time and circumstance can alter judgment, regardless of one's knowledge of the field. Seeing Chaplin's *Monsieur Verdoux* as a young man, for example, I was certain it was a masterpiece; returning to it twenty years later, I could hardly remain awake until the final frame. And lest you think my opinions are affected only by the passage of years, I should confess that I had diametrically opposite impressions of Mel Brooks's *Young Frankenstein* within weeks of seeing it first with older friends and then with my eleven-year-old son. Chastened by these experiences, I have come to believe that the least valuable criticism is that composed of naked assertions of taste (the kind Danny Kaye parodied when, being asked how he liked the Himalayas, he replied "Loved him! Hated her!"). And that is why critics with an ambition to be remembered have poured so much energy into analysis and commentary in the hope that their perceptions might somehow outlive their opinions.

Still, the opinions of a critic informed with taste and learning are likely to be more accurate, in the long run, than those of a journalist recruited for theatre reviewing because he can write fast—which makes it remarkable that those who report on theatre for TV and the newspapers should have gained so much influence over the fate of the New York stage. It is even more remarkable, considering how few of the theatre reviewers associated with the media possess the kind of authority in the field that would explain their power—the authority, say, of Hilton Kramer in art or Pauline Kael in film or Andrew Porter in music, to name only those working in mass-circulation newspapers and magazines. Clearly, in the case of the theatre, the power to make or break a play resides not in the individual but in the position: It is conferred by the institution for which he works. If you doubt this, consider how quickly Walter Kerr's influence as daily reviewer for the New York *Times* passed to Clive Barnes when Kerr left that position to write for the Sunday Arts and Leisure section; consider also how much less impact Kerr has had on the economics of the theatre as a weekly reviewer, even though his reviews have remained substantially the same in quality and concern. Under such circumstances, it is understandable why people often ask, before they decide to go to a play, not so much what Barnes thought but "What did the *Times* have to say?"

That the *Times,* as an institution, should have anything to say in judgment of a theatrical work strikes me as incompatible with its claim to be an organ of the news, which is to say an impartial journal of facts. For it is within this journalistic imperative that the *Times* has always insisted on reviewing all plays the morning after opening, on the premise that an opening night is a news event, to be covered as quickly as a labor strike or a plane crash. Still, where the news of the day is generally reported in a relatively factual manner, with judgments reserved for the editorial page, the news of the theatre is replete with instant opinions and subjective impressions, the reviewers offering their personal views to the reader as if they were established facts. (This tendency to confuse surmises with certainties is exacerbated by the format of the newspaper which gives each review a headline containing not a straightforward description of the event but rather the reviewer's judgment of value.) I am not suggesting that the news media should refrain from covering the theatre—but to be consistent with their claims, TV and newspapers would have to treat each opening night *literally* as a news event, telling us who was responsible for the show, who was in the audience, what accidents occurred outside the theatre, and anything else that could be objectively reported. Thus, the headline of a review (say, ALBEE'S NEW PLAY LIGHTS UP BROADWAY) would be adapted to something a little less arguable as an idea (say, JACKIE ONASSIS ATTENDS NEW ALBEE PLAY IN HALSTON KAFTAN), and the reputation for objectivity cherished by the news media could be better preserved.

I have no illusion that this proposal will be taken seriously —I'm not even very serious about it myself. I bring it up mainly in order to illustrate my conviction that the newspaper and TV reviewers derive their power, and derive it mostly illegitimately, from the news context in which they function. Obviously, opinions will continue to dominate these reviews because readers have been conditioned to look for them; and there is no doubt that the reviewer's likes and dislikes constitute the most lively, if most forgettable, aspect of his notice. On the other hand, I am convinced that something will have to be done to demythologize the writers who now arbitrate the hits and flops of the New York stage, and this will not be accomplished until theatregoers are somehow persuaded that many valid opinions can obtain about a theatrical work, including the ones they hold themselves. Perhaps the solution for a paper like the *Times* is to publish two simultaneous reviews of each production side by side, for then, even if both reviewers agreed, there would no longer be the sense that a journal held a single house position about a play.

None of these suggestions would be necessary had not theatre reviewing fallen almost entirely to the news media by default. But it is a melancholy fact that the kind of reflective criticism formerly practiced in the weekly, monthly, and quarterly journals has virtually disappeared. Where theatre used to attract thinkers of the quality of Stark Young, Eric Bentley, Francis Fergusson, Kenneth Tynan, Richard Gilman, Wilfrid Sheed, Richard Hayes, Albert Bermel, Stanley Kauffmann, Harold Clurman, Elizabeth Hardwick, Susan Sontag, Mary McCarthy, and the like, only a very small number of these are still reviewing plays and then only irregularly, while such magazines as the *New York Review, Partisan Review,* the *New Republic, Harper's* and the *New Leader* have either abandoned their theatre coverage or drastically reduced its space. (The *Village Voice,* furthermore, which used to devote almost half the paper to theatre reviews, has now cut back to a few columns.) It could be argued that a decline of this sort merely reflects a decline in the quality of the stage—except that it has been occurring at precisely the moment when a group of theatres has emerged in this country which at last might be considered worthy of serious intellectual scrutiny.

In fact, it was partly in response to the appeal of these alternative critics that the alternative theatre came into being, in order to feed an appetite for theatrical art that was not being satisfied by Broadway. Such institutional resident theatres as the Mark Taper, the Chelsea Theatre Center, the Guthrie, the Folger, the New York Public Theatre, the Open Theatre, the American Place Theatre, the Long Wharf, the Trinity Square Playhouse, the Yale Repertory Theatre, Cafe La Mama, the Manhattan Project, and many others were developed, to one degree or another, in reply to the critical demand for more attention to process, for decentralization, for experiment and risk, for continuity of purpose, for ensemble work, for adventurous programing, for poetic and thoughtful approaches— the demand, in short, that the American theatre begin to display the kind of artistic sensibilities that were currently being found in the American novel, painting, music, dance, and poetry. Granted, many of these ambitions were not immediately realized, but that was hardly surprising considering how long the stage had been dominated by commercial concepts. The very idea of a national art theatre movement in America was so unusual that it took time to seep down into the minds of audiences and practitioners alike.

And now that this idea has just begun to take root in the cultural imagination, the intelligent eye that might have evaluated its results has decided to close. For the alternative critics, long the most vocal opponents of Broadway's tawdry glamour and cheap commercialism, have abandoned the theatre at its crucial moment—and not because the theatre has ceased to be interesting but, one suspects, because it has ceased to be chic. What other explanation accounts for the singular indifference so many of these writers have shown toward the young experimental American playwrights, the innovative directors, the actors with the capacity to transform themselves from role to role instead of repeating old tricks, the designers who have made such imaginative departures from the box set, indeed, the very companies which annually risk their existence with unusual presentations? It was easy enough to attack the pretensions of Broadway's "serious" drama, its fake masterpieces and manufactured hits, but where was the curiosity that might have propelled these people, once Broadway stopped providing targets for their scorn, into boroughs outside of Manhattan and cities beyond New York? Where was the questing spirit, the lust for art, the impulse to discover achievement wherever it arose, that presumably attracted them to theatre criticism in the first place?

Well, it seems to have evaporated. With a few honorable exceptions most of the alternative critics have preferred to stay home. To speak from personal experience is to mention all those unanswered letters and unreturned phone calls, all those broken promises and canceled appointments, all those requests for limousines to and from New Haven, after invitations had been issued to people I respected to come see some special production I thought might excite their interest. One of those who never paid us a visit in all nine years of our existence was the critic for an intellectual monthly, a bright former playwright, who, during a recent symposium in his magazine, volunteered the opinion that "so far as drama is concerned, public support of culture has put up about 25 terrible repertory companies throughout the country. But what else?" Since this critic had never, on the evidence of his reviews, ventured to a theatre more than a hundred blocks' distance from Elaine's restaurant in New York, I wrote to him immediately, saying that I was preparing this article and asking him the following questions: "1) How many of these companies have you visited? 2) How many productions by these companies have you seen? 3) How many of these productions have you reviewed?" I was not surprised to receive no reply.

Well, this critic is entitled to whatever opinion he wants to express, just as he is free to say that the twenty-five companies in the country (actually there are fifty-five) are "terrible." But whatever the basis for such views, criticism of this kind is worthless to the resident theatre movement—as worthless as the criticism which lavishes on these theatres unstinting praise.

And worse than worthless, it is deeply disappointing. I speak as an obvious partisan, with a stake in training and production for nonprofit theatres, when I say that it was the hope of the repertory movement that it would begin to attract repertory critics—which is to say, writers with the capacity to judge not just individual productions but the design and purpose of the whole. Such critics would have journeyed anywhere, as only the *Times* reviewers seem able to do at present, in their search for meaningful theatrical experiences—eager to observe and analyze the progress of theatre artists from production to production under the auspices of organic company work. Critics of this kind might have functioned as the conscience of the American theatre as an institution, identifying what the purpose of a company was and when it departed from that purpose, when it compromised its identity and for what reasons. Such critics would have been discriminating, even harsh, but they would have known that the language of hyperbolic praise and vitriolic dispraise was the equipment of the commercial critic for establishing hits and flops (and stars and scapegoats), not for describing purposeful works of art or the progress of artists. They would have known that beyond their value judgments was the need for interpretation, imaginative description, comparative analysis, and keeping an accurate record of what they had seen.

Alas, such critics never materialized, and partly as a result, many good theatres have begun to lose their way. Does anyone doubt whether Joe Papp would have abandoned his determination to produce new plays at Lincoln Center in the face of a hostile audience and a hostile press if—regardless of the quality of individual productions—just one authoritative critic had understood and supported his general policy? The pressures on the nonprofit theatres to conform to audience tastes are simply enormous, and at the moment, the critical fraternity is largely following this taste rather than trying to lead it. If you want to know why so many committed theatre people seem so despondent at the present moment, just take a moment to examine the reviews. The advances of the American stage are being written on water, and nobody is keeping an intelligent record of what has been achieved.

(1975)

TWO

John Simon (Uneasy Stages *and* Singularities)

IT IS COMMON knowledge that American culture has produced at least two John Simons: "John Simon the Good," who makes his living in publishing, giving editorial support and encouragement to creative people, and "John Simon the Bad," who makes his living in criticism, giving other sorts of creative people bilious attacks and nervous disorders. After reading through these two collections of theatre essays and reviews, I have become convinced that the critical John Simon is composed of divided *personae* as well, which, for convenience' sake, we'll call the good, the bad, and the ugly.

The ugly side of this writer has by now become almost legendary, and it is generously displayed in the bulkier of these two books—*Uneasy Stages,* Simon's collected theatre reviews (mostly for *New York* magazine) between 1963 and 1973. As one who covered many of the same productions during a similar period, I can testify to the ordeal suffered by Simon during a bleak decade of the New York theatre. But this only partially explains his compulsion to retaliate against his putative tor-

mentors by pouring personal insult on their heads. Mr. Simon
—curiously exultant over having alienated almost the entire
theatrical community with his lacerating attacks—takes note in
his preface that he is continually being called "acerbic":
"Why," he asks, "can't I sometimes be called the barbed,
biting, acidulous, peppery, sharp, tart or sardonic John
Simon?"

None of these adjectives, including "acerbic," is an inappro-
priate description of his style, but unfortunately its most vivid
component is comething considerably less appealing—mur-
derous brutality. Judicious enough in analyzing literature,
John Simon apparently goes ape whenever he sees a moving
object; as a result, he has become the chosen journalist of
those who, in earlier times, would have found their pleasure
in bearbaiting or pigsticking. No matter how cogent his analysis—and he is sometimes perceptive in the extreme—no matter how accurate his judgments—and his batting average is as
high as that of any critic of the period—he almost invariably
unbalances his reviews with a vituperative assault on the morbid failings of some playwright, director, or other critic, and
particularly on the "flipper-like limbs" or "tuberous left
breast" of some hapless actress whose personal appearance
has violated his aesthetic sense. "There must be beauty in the
theatre," he cries, making it perfectly clear that he means
physical beauty—"spiritual beauty," he says, "is not all that
useful to an actress" because "it is a slow worker."

This is unconvincing to say the least. Like the literary figure
he most resembles—Molière's misanthropic Alceste—Simon
is given to rationalizing his prejudices, and this paean to
beauty sounds like the self-deception of an oddly glamour-
dazed, stage-door sensibility. Nor does it explain the wild
gusto with which he assails the exterior qualities of such good
actresses as Maureen Stapleton and Zoë Caldwell. Simon identifies what he calls his "wrath" as a passion, not a failing, but
this *saevo indignatio* does not, as the true satirist's must, spare
the persons while speaking the vices. His prose is most ener-

getic and charged when it is most caustic and personal, and the longest pieces in this collection are usually inspired by the things he most loathes. Simon defends himself by asserting that he who loves well chastises well, claiming that other reviewers, myself included, have been equally harsh, though perhaps more sorrowful. If this is true, then I hereby publicly apologize. Were this the only record of American performance during the period, actors would be remembered primarily for their glazed eyes, warts, bad skin, and rotten teeth.

Having faulted the ugly John Simon for his intemperate personal attacks, I would blame the bad John Simon for his critical failings and stylistic lapses. Simon is extremely learned, but he is not one to wear his learning lightly. For a writer so sensitive to faulty translation and grammatical abominations (he shudders at "the horrid neologism 'anymore' in the title of Tennessee Williams' latest play"), Simon seems oddly unconscious of the excesses in his own prose, which is riddled with puns, word quibbles, Latinisms, and pedantries. Often precise and witty, Simon will just as often go into painful contortions in order to set up a trope (as in his elaborate description of a "baked-Alaska performance" by "Scott of the Antarctic"), and naked assertions of taste too frequently substitute for reflective analysis or discussion of ideas. Simon has strong opinions on virtually every subject. He seems never to be in doubts or uncertainties, which leaves one with the impression that he is not particularly open to experience—or, for that matter, to certain vital forms of theatre, such as American farce and satire.

John Simon's bad and ugly features are prominent enough —in fact, they have made him famous. But it would be a pity if the savagery and arrogance that brought him the attention of the media were to obscure his real virtues, which he is often in danger of ignoring himself. These virtues can be found in his slim volume of theatre essays, *Singularities,* for in these leisurely pieces, written for more sedentary occasions than review deadlines, Simon emerges as a drama critic of genuine distinction, one who preserved his scholarship, courage, clear-sightedness, and capacity for outrage when most of those around were losing theirs.

Simon's scholarship is amply displayed whenever he discusses plays rather than performances—and especially in two exemplary articles on the structure of *Peer Gynt* and the eye imagery of *The Wild Duck*. There, his affectionate understanding of the works of Henrik Ibsen proves equal, in my opinion, to that of any modern commentator. Simon characterizes such essays, in his preface, as "what I might do for a hobby, as against what I do in the line of duty," thus suggesting that if he ever stopped playing the role of spitting critic, he might relax happily into a learned exegete of Germanic texts, and one possessed of surprising generosity. This is not to say that *Singularities* is free of Simon's characteristic ferocity, but rather that this quality seems more fully controlled in his essays than in his reviews. And he has remained almost unique in his courageous refusal, despite fierce ideological pressure, to overestimate black and countercultural plays, as well as in his capacity to withstand the fashionable frauds of the theatre at the very moment that they were being foisted on the public by our cultural brokers.

In this regard, I would recommend his remarks on the antihuman implications buried in such quaint fads as Happenings ("This is laboring under the delusion that humanism has outlived itself, when in fact the only trouble with it is that it has not yet caught on"), on the Broadway nostalgia cult ("The very etymology indicates that it is not a good thing; a pain, a sickness, whose cure may not exist"), and on the indiscriminate enshrinement of the new by trend-hungry writers ("The avant-garde is acceptable because it is essentially reactionary, harmless . . . the dead center, the very Establishment"). And although I believe his repudiation of the Polish Laboratory Theater to be excessive and ultimately wrongheaded, it is a refreshing corrective to those who announced the arrival of Jerzy Grotowski as a kind of theatrical Second Coming, bringing a stage scripture composed no longer of language but of arcane gesture.

Because Simon's ideas in *Singularities* are more predominant than his personality, he is provocative there even when you disagree with him—as I do frequently over his insensitivity to the performance process, his over-lofty view of criticism, and his unexamined conviction that a pluralistic, ethnocentric, racially divided, sexually split society like the United States could or should have a National Theatre (how can you have a "National Theatre" until you have a nation?).

Still, when Simon allows himself to be good, he is very, very good. Extreme in tone and method, even in *Singularities,* Simon has been virtually alone in his effort to preserve some standards in a debased form—and when you consider all the weaseling, fudging, flakking, boosting, pettifogging, and downright lying that pass these days for theatre criticism, Simon emerges as a paragon of candor, almost a voice in the wilderness.

For that reason, the thoughtful essayist of *Singularities* makes us even more indignant about the sadistic showman of *Uneasy Stages*—and it makes us reflect, too, on how American culture invariably picks up what is coarse and extroverted about our literary figures for the sake of its entertainment. Simon's development into the Transylvanian vampire of *New York* magazine, his fangs dripping every week with fresh blood, represents the progress of a figure who might have made considerable contributions had he been able to resist the pulls of his editors, his admirers, and his own nature. At the moment, however, the reflective critic is being eclipsed by the scurrilous public performer, and the worser qualities of the man are in the ascendant.

(1976)

THREE

Pauline Kael (Reeling)

IF IT WERE possible to choose a single characteristic that accounts for Pauline Kael's animation and charm as a movie reviewer, I would say it is her irrepressible enthusiasm. At a time when many critics of the arts are expressing feelings of dejection, even a sense of apocalypse about their subjects, Miss Kael continues to write about movies with the breathless delirium of one smitten with young love. Always poised to recognize achievement, she is as eager to embrace talent as some others are to revile it, and even when she dislikes a film, she still manages to convey her unshakable devotion to the movie medium.

This is not to suggest that Miss Kael is undiscriminating—actually, she can be the most tough-minded of critics. But since reason and love keep little company together nowadays, she will frequently throw away caution for the sake of a momentary crush. It is remarkable how, after twenty years of reviewing, she has been able to sustain the same keen appetite for celluloid fantasy, the same intense interest in movie stars, as the most avid Hollywood fan. She correctly divines, in fact, that attractions of this kind are fundamental to moviegoing, and admits to sharing with her readers an almost sensual participation in the life of the screen.

The erotic components of Miss Kael's relationship to the movies are suggested in the titles of her collections—*I Lost It At the Movies; Kiss, Kiss, Bang, Bang; Deeper Into Movies; All the Way With Movies*—and they are implicit in the dizzy pun that constitutes the title of her latest book, *Reeling.* In the foreword to this work—a compendium of reviews written, mostly for *The New Yorker* magazine, between 1972 and 1975—she makes some of these associations explicit by contrasting what she calls the "sensual starvation" of the stage with the "erotic potential" of the films, "the constant flow of imagery, the quick shifts of place, the sudden rush of feeling." "There's a reason," she observes, "for that 'Wow!' which often seems all that a person can say after coming out of a movie house"—movies provide "an excitement that is a great high . . . they can give us almost everything, almost anything."

This somewhat overheated claim begins to suggest how deeply this writer identifies her own responses with those of other moviegoers. An intellectual who is not afraid of sensation, she is probably more in tune with the popular audience than any other serious American reviewer. Pauline Kael hardly sees herself as an adversary critic. Indeed, when she feels compelled to apologize for past errors, it is not for making critical misjudgments but rather for failing to sympathize sufficiently with the needs of mass taste—for "dismissing big, bludgeoning movies without realizing how much they might mean to people, rejecting humid sentiment and imagining that no one could be affected by it."

It is hard not to admire this kind of generosity, and it is likely that these warm, democratic convictions make possible the conversational felicities of her style—that sassy, breezy, gabby vernacular prose which makes you feel like you've been personally buttonholed by a wonderfully knowledgeable companion who won't let go of your lapel until she has persuaded you one way or another about a film. Miss Kael's relaxed relations with the reader also account for the easy flow of her wit, with its high quota of spontaneity and its low content of malice. Not least among the pleasures of *Reeling* is to come upon her capsule put-downs of meretricious movies like *Day of the Dolphin* ("the most expensive Rin Tin Tin movie ever made") or of vaguely narcissistic actors like Robert Redford ("has turned almost alarmingly blond—he's gone platinum, he must be into plutonium; his hair is coordinated with his teeth").

This description of Redford suggests another characteristic of Miss Kael's criticism—her preoccupation with the physical look of actors. At her best, she is able to write about the human face as if it were the equivalent of a moral act. She is also capable, at her worst, of Hollywood groupie gush, as when she loses her heart to Shelley Duvall ("You go right to her in delight, saying 'I'm yours' ") or—though this infatuation later cools—when she falls head over heels for Barbra Streisand ("the greatest camera subject on the contemporary American scene"). At times, too, she gets so lost in her work that she seems to have no reference points outside of films. It is disturbing to see her wasting elaborate descriptive resources in comparing a stiff like Cybill Shepherd with her zombie predecessor, Gloria Grahame ("Shepherd doesn't have Grahame's marvelous trashiness, or her acting control either, but she has aroused the same vindictive masculinity," etc.). At moments like this, her language becomes indistinguishable from the conversation one might overhear between two women exchanging movie magazines under the hair dryer.

Miss Kael's populist sympathies, however, permit her to confess something that the more highbrow film critics are sometimes inclined to conceal or ignore—namely, that movies can be enjoyed on the "shameless levels" of mindless entertainment. Her own capacity for popcorn escapism may explain how she can write at length on such forgettable items as *Young Winston* ("can be enjoyed on its own junk terms") or *Lady Sings the Blues* ("factually, it's a fraud, but emotionally it delivers"), and why she never seems to lose her zest even when enlarging on such bonehead material as *The Poseidon Adventure* ("the script is the true cataclysm") or *The Towering Inferno* ("has opened just in time to capture the Dumb Whore Award of 1974"). The only kind of film, in fact, that really turns her off is the big, brutal juggernaut like *Dirty Harry* or *Magnum Force* —not because it is violent, but rather because it is "emotionless" in its violence, and thereby manipulates the latent thug sensibilities of the average moviegoer.

Miss Kael is extremely protective of the average moviegoer, who, she feels, is being persistently victimized, along with the serious American director, by the studio moguls. And in the single think piece included in the present volume—a long essay called "On the Future of Movies"—she blisters the Hollywood system both for debasing its audience and ignoring its artists. Miss Kael, displaying a touching faith in the box-office appeal of serious new films, is convinced that big producers are hostile to good directors not because they are uncommercial, but because they make the businessmen uncomfortable. And for this reason, they promote slick formula hits at the expense of meritorious works of art, underestimating the moviegoer and demoralizing the director. "The directors spend their lives not in learning their craft but in fighting a battle they keep losing . . . A fatal difference between the 'high' arts and the popular, or mass-culture, arts has been that in one the artist's mistakes are his own, while in the other the mistakes are largely the businessman's."

Pauline Kael has worked gallantly and tirelessly to correct these mistakes. She has been an enthusiastic partisan of American filmmakers like Francis Ford Coppola, Martin Scorsese, Paul Mazursky, and Robert Altman, most of whom have tried to work inside the Hollywood system without sacrificing their personal vision. Her support for their films has been partly motivated by a desire to influence "the decisions of the movie companies about what will sell and what won't"—to prove, in short, that the sensibilities of the average moviegoer are sufficiently large to accommodate new experimental work. If there are disadvantages to her generosity and enthusiasm, they lie, I think, in the way her concern over the promotion and distribution of the films she likes has begun to cloud her aesthetic judgments of them.

For her writing is becoming larded with hyperbole. To judge from *Reeling,* the movie world has been delivering a masterpiece almost every week—a masterpiece not only perfect in itself but supreme in its genre. *The Godfather* is "the greatest gangster picture ever made"; *The Long Goodbye* is "probably the best American movie ever made that didn't open in New York"; *Don't Look Back* is "the fanciest, most carefully assembled gothic enigma yet put on screen"; *Mean Streets* is "a true original of the period, a triumph of personal film-making"; *Thieves Like Us* is "the closest to flawless of Altman's films—a masterpiece"; *Shampoo* is "the most virtuoso example of sophisticated, kaleidoscopic farce that American moviemakers have ever come up with"; *Nashville* is "the funniest epic version of America ever to reach the screen" . . . this sort of thing has begun to multiply out of all proportion to anything in her previous work.

I don't mean to quarrel with Miss Kael's opinions. I enjoyed most of these movies myself, and anyway, even were she to prove an unreliable guide, "bad taste" (as she says herself in another context) "isn't the worst thing in the world." No, what disturbs me about these quotes is the promotional quality of the language, and the way her enthusiasm is just beginning to fade over from partisanship into press agentry. Like most influential critics, Miss Kael must be aware that she is writing not only for the reader, but for the advertising agency—movie ads now reprint her reviews sometimes in their entirety—but in her wholly laudable efforts to bring good movies to the attention of as many people as possible, she has, willy-nilly, become a cog in the marketing mechanism of the very system she deplores.

Although this may be beyond her control, her impulse to proclaim instant masterpieces is not, and the fragility of Miss Kael's hyperbolic claims is nowhere better illustrated than in her notorious review of *Last Tango in Paris.* Bertolucci's film, a sensitive exploration of sexual despair distinguished by a fine performance from Marlo Brando, seems to have released every extravagance in Miss Kael's vocabulary of superlatives. With this film, she writes, "The movie breakthrough has finally come . . . Bertolucci and Brando have altered the face of an art form." It is both "the most powerfully erotic movie ever made" and "the most liberating movie ever made." The date of its appearance at the New York Film Festival "should become a landmark in movie history comparable to . . . the night *Le Sacre du Printemps* was first performed in music history." The film "has made the strongest impression on me in almost twenty years of reviewing. This is a movie people will be arguing about, I think, for as long as there are movies."

One has no reason to doubt the genuineness of Miss Kael's response here, but the sad thing about these assertions is that today nobody seems to be arguing about *Last Tango in Paris:* It was pretty much ingested, absorbed and forgotten a few months after its release (there was more argument, significantly, over Miss Kael's review). One of the difficulties with a sensation-hungry culture like our own is that it moves too fast to establish "landmarks," and criticism which pumps up weekly masterpieces, like so many inflatable balloons, simply further excites the nervous media atmosphere of our time. I admire Pauline Kael's courage in taking unqualified positions, and I understand the need for a young, somewhat insecure medium like the movies to establish its "breakthroughs." But great works of art are likely to appear as infrequently in film as in any other art form, and it is no service to those rare exhalations that very occasionally make themselves visible to identify all the minor nebulae as blazing comets.

For these reasons—because it is so full of "masterpieces," because it is so full of kitsch—*Reeling* ultimately grinds you down. It is always an entertaining book, and piece by piece a brilliant one, but taking it in large doses, you may get frazzled by all the feverish energy, flashing like St. Elmo's fire, around so many ephemeral works. Perhaps because the movies *are* a sensual medium, they are more likely to provoke hot, opinionated responses than cool, disinterested ideas, and without sufficient intellectual substance, the continual play of even such a fine sensibility around an impure object eventually gets tiresome. (By interesting contrast, she is always intellectually stimulating when writing about the products of the "sensually starved" theatre.)

Pauline Kael's greatest virtues are the source of her defects: Her desire to introduce the serious film to large popular audiences involves her too much in its merchandising; her stake in reforming the industry tends to implicate her in the commercial system; her enthusiasm occasionally affects her detachment; her movie high sometimes keeps her insulated from the world beyond the screening room. Somewhere in *Reeling,* she mentions that reading some writers is "close to the pleasure of the movies." Reading Pauline Kael's *Reeling* is close to that pleasure as well, but if you're interested in thoughts and images other than those produced by celluloid, you might be wise to savor those delights a little at a time.

(1976)

FOUR

===

H. L. Mencken (The New Mencken Letters)

SINCE H. L. MENCKEN has hardly been a fashionable journalist during the twenty years following his death in 1956, it is unlikely that the publication of his correspondence will inspire massive interest. Nevertheless, this new volume of Mencken letters—affectionately edited with an excellent biographical commentary by Carl Bode, professor of American literature at the University of Maryland—is something of a minor event in American cultural history, and a major one in the history of the American personality.

Reading over the thousand or so letters (selected from over a hundred thousand) that Mencken wrote to various friends and correspondents in his terse, unbuttoned style, one can easily see why this Baltimore ruffian has fallen out of favor. Oozing with prejudice—equally spread between Communists and puritans, between uneducated "boobs" and teacher's-college "quacks," between Comstocks, fundamentalists, and Roosevelt New Dealers—Mencken also runs over with simple dislike for Jews, blacks, Poles, teetotalers, and dogs (he gets especially incensed over the defilement of his beloved Union Square by defecating and copulating canines). If this makes him sound like the W. C. Fields of journalism, then that may be the most felicitous way to regard him today, for his prejudices—proudly self-acknowledged and even published in a series of volumes by that name—are often hard to forgive in the light of recent history.

Mencken's Teutonic ancestry and affinities, for example, not only made him sympathetic to Germany's military policy during World War I but also blinded him for a long while to the true nature of Hitler and the Third Reich. In 1919 it may still have been possible to joke away one's dislike for Freudianism by wishing that its author "as a Jew . . . will fall victim to some obscure race war in Vienna," but as late as 1941, when that jest was already a horrible actuality, Mencken was writing (to James T. Farrell) that "Hitler's history will follow that of Bonaparte . . . He will be denounced violently as a moral leper while he lives, but after his death judgment will be revised and he will come to be a sort of hero." Even in 1942 Mencken, while rejecting Hitler's ideas, was still insisting that "the German scheme is working better than Roosevelt's half orthodox and half Communist American scheme." (Despite his hatred of authoritarianism, he was similarly attracted to Mussolini's Italy: "Everything is clean, the roads are superb, even at Pompeii the guides stand back"—a classic example of the tourist impressed by the Fascist capacity to make the trains run on time.)

If Mencken's political judgments were often bad, his political prophecies were even worse. In 1936—the same year he predicted Alf Landon's victory over Roosevelt—he announced that there would be no European war because "the German Army was not prepared," while expressing his "low opinion of Russia as a military power." A lousy prophet and a part-time bigot, Mencken managed simultaneously to be a confirmed civil libertarian and a staunch defender of free expression. What saved him was his philosophical anarchism: "The simple truth," he writes, "is that I detest all movements and all uplift-ers," meaning ideologues of every stripe, orthodoxies of every persuasion. Hating Marxism, he nevertheless fought to pre-vent Emma Goldman's deportation to the Soviet Union. Loathing Communists—not to mention those liberals who supported their rights in the United States while rationalizing the suppression of civil liberties in Russia—he nevertheless defended their presence in the university.

Mencken, in short, was often able to subordinate his preju-dices to his principles, though he usually tried to accommo-date both. "I have always been in favor," he writes to Gerald W. Johnson in 1947, "of giving [Communists] the utmost free-dom, but I should add that I believe in the long run it will be necessary to butcher them . . . When they work their nuisance value to the point when they begin to be unendurable the only recourse is to put them to death." Indeed, one of the remark-able things about Mencken is the contrast between his passion for the public weal and his bristling, often exaggerated hostili-ties. While his correspondence is larded with disparaging ref-erences to black people, he was an implacable foe of the Ku Klux Klan and lynching, and wrote his last article on behalf of integration, attacking the Maryland authorities who had ar-rested a group of blacks and whites in the act of trying to integrate a tennis court.

Still, Mencken is at his most vivid not as a thinker or critic, but rather as a comic personality, a rowdy human being. The contempt he felt toward the mass of humanity ("Obviously, the human race," he writes, "is both ignorant and vicious . . . It is actually no more virtuous than a gang of rats") was more than compensated for by the warmth, generosity, and loyalty he expressed toward his friends—and for those rough-neck authors, like Dreiser, Farrell, and Henry Miller, whom he championed against such paleskins as Henry James. His feel-ings for women, while rarely tender, were always courteous and delicate, and the letters chronicle his deep despondency over the loss of his wife, Sara, who died of tuberculosis within five years of their marriage. But it was as a saloon companion that he found his true fulfillment, and it was in the consumption of malt liquor that he found his chief delight.

Indeed, I do not think it excessive to say that, apart from his interest in language, his pleasure in beer was the stimulus for his greatest excitement and his greatest expertise. Mencken's gift for tracking down the etymology of American words, in preparation for his books and supplements on the subject, inspired a couple of hilarious letters—one in which he badgers an undertaker over the origin of the word "mortician," another in which he speculates on the history of the slang term for *pudendum muliebre.* But the classics in this collection are those comic Prohibition epics in which Mencken expresses his fury over the Volstead Act and relates his misadventures in pursuit of the mysteries of the home brew:

"Last Sunday I manufactured five gallons of Methodistbrau. It turned out to be very tasty, as Dreiser would say, but I bottled it too soon, and the result has been a series of fearful explosions. Last night I had three quart bottles in my side yard, cooling in a bucket. Two went off at once, bringing my neighbor out of his house with yells. He thought the Soviets had seized the town. I have lost about 12 good Apollinaris bottles but still trust in God. Next time I shall wait until the fermentation is finished. Just now another blew up in my cellar . . . I shall make dandelion wine if I can find a dandelion. But down here they are not to be trusted. Dogs always piss on them. And, now and then, a policeman."

This pretty much gives the flavor of the man and of his exuberant style: yeasty, bubbling, tangy, slightly bitter, explosive—at one with his bootlegged brew. Like W. C. Fields—indeed, like most great comic personalities in the Falstaffian tradition—Mencken represents what George Orwell called "the voice of the belly protesting against the soul," the unofficial self that is as much a part of every human being as codes of sacrifice and tolerance. In that sense, Mencken's prejudices, his bigotry, his aggressiveness, and his bile are almost essential to his *persona,* as they are surely the sources of much of his comic genius.

A watchdog age devoted to ending injustice, equalizing opportunity, and protecting wounded sensibilities is not likely to be very responsive to such a figure, and Mencken—once "the most powerful personal influence on this whole generation of educated people," according to Walter Lippmann—is now virtually a forgotten man. Each era manages to correct the excesses of the preceding period while creating its own mistakes, and it may be that in our oversensitivity to defamation and bigotry, we are losing a necessary antidote to hypocrisy, piety, exaggerated scruples, and official virtue, perhaps even detouring intolerance into more subterranean, dangerous avenues.

At any rate, Mencken has left no heirs and has barely survived himself. As he wrote somewhat plaintively in 1943, "The life of every man who dissents from prevailing ideas is bound to be more or less lonely." His own posthumous loneliness is partially a reflection on our own conformist times, and partially, of course, well deserved. Unregenerate and probably damned, he is certainly not sitting among the saints. But wherever he is, I hope he is accompanied by pneumatic maidens, good Bach music, Havana cigars, and strong Pilsner beer.

(1976)

FIVE

Tennessee Williams (Letters to Donald Windham: 1940–1965)

IF REVENGE is a dish that tastes best cold, then Donald Windham has certainly fixed himself a satisfying frozen dinner. He has published all the letters sent to him between 1940 and 1965 by Tennessee Williams ("the rarest, the most intoxicating, the most memorable flower that has blossomed in my garden of good and evil," he calls him in an introduction), and without ever losing his poise as a reticent editor and admiring friend, has allowed the glorious bird to dip his own tail feathers in a pot of tar.

Most of these letters were written during the 1940s, when Williams and Windham were collaborating on a stage adaptation of a D. H. Lawrence story called "You Touched Me!" Although the idea for the project originates with Windham, Williams quickly perceives its commercial possibilities, and the correspondence documents the playwright's increasing involvement in the work, and—as his fame spreads—his increasing expropriation of credit and royalties. Before long, this "perfect friend," as Williams continues to call him, has allowed his collaborator's name to be removed from the publicity releases, has permitted his agent to try to reduce his portion of the potential take, and if we are to believe Windham's footnotes, has effectively excluded him from participation in the production of the play. (It fails anyway, putting additional strains on the relationship.)

One more ill-fated collaboration takes place between them, when Williams undertakes to direct Windham's play, *The Starless Air,* in Houston. During this period, Windham finds himself barred from the rehearsals of his own work, only to discover later that Williams has taken the liberty of rewriting some of his speeches (introducing references to "mendacity" that are later to appear in *Cat on a Hot Tin Roof*). The entire project collapses when Williams can't find the time to direct the play on Broadway.

Stretched by these tokens of human devotedness, the friendship between the two men frays and tears, though it never actually unravels. The letters grow more guarded, more defensive, more infrequent, finally concluding in the 1960s, after Windham has published a *roman à clef* which he intends as a tribute to Williams but which the playwright takes badly. Later, Williams gives his friend permission to sell a *Glass Menagerie* manuscript to support his sojourn in Rome, but even this generous gesture causes acrimony, since Williams does not realize a sufficiently large tax break from the sale: "The manuscript," Windham writes, "went for $6000—considerably less than the $10,000 he expected—and I was soon hearing that I had sold it the wrong way and cost him a great deal of money."

Throughout the quarter-century of mistreatment chronicled in the book, Windham maintains an air of sympathetic understanding, in a display of what Williams characterizes as his "morbid humility." The yeast of hurt feelings, however, has fermented enough in the meantime to rise subtly in the publication of this private correspondence, where Williams emerges as a figure with no apparent interest in anything but the advancement of his career and the satisfaction of his appetites. Gore Vidal, reviewing Williams' autobiographical *Me-moirs,* has remarked on the playwright's "indifference to place, art, history"; his observation is more than confirmed in the Windham letters.

Indeed, it is remarkable—considering Williams' creative sensitivity in his plays—how little he actually permits himself to *see* on his travels abroad. He finds no "charm" in Paris except for "three lovely clubs where the boys dance together." He is "forlorn" in London because "there are only middle-aged fags who still think they are young and pretty." He adores Rome, primarily because "you can't walk a block without being accosted by someone you would spend a whole evening trying to make in the New York bars." The threat of a Communist takeover in Italy is a source of apprehension because it might result in the deportation of Americans like himself at a time when "the boys are beginning to put on shorts and the days are a succession of gold."

Landscape, architecture, nature, food, politics, philosophy, the social climate—none of these arouse much commentary from Williams, or assume much importance, as compared with that long parade of hustlers, rough trade, sailors, and young boys that cruise through his waking and dreaming life like so many wind-up toys. As in *Memoirs,* this book shows a man inordinately, obsessively preoccupied with announcing his erotic adventures—a concern that is eclipsed, and only mo-mentarily, by his hypochondriacal worries over his health. The love that previously dared not speak its name has now grown hoarse from screaming it.

Still, the really significant thing in these pages for biogra-phers, analysts, and just plain literary gossips is not Williams erotomania, but rather his treatment of friends and acquaint-ances, for this provides the most revealing and, let us admit it, the most amusing passages of the book. Although Williams expresses impatience with Truman Capote's "callous sort of bitchery," he has a pretty impressive gift himself for planting teeth in another's back. When he meets Gore Vidal, for example, he professes to be "crazy" about him ("A beauty and only 23"), but one month later, he is saying: "I liked him but only through the strenuous effort it took to overlook his conceit. He has studied ballet and is constantly doing pirouettes and flexing his legs, and the rest of the time he is comparing himself and Truman Capote . . . to such figures as Dostoevsky and Balzac." Leonard Bernstein, whom he meets in Mexico and later extols in *Memoirs,* is characterized as "nice, but, oh, what an egoist! When not getting all the attention, he sits in a chair with closed eyes, pretending to be asleep." And he is priceless on such child stars as Margaret O'Brien, whom he encountered in Hollywood while trying to work up a movie for Lana Turner: "If you are lucky, you haven't seen her. She is a small and more loathsome edition of Shirley Temple before *that* one retired from the screen. I do indeed have a story for her, but it is unprintable."

Less entertaining is the tendency, already seen in his relationship with Windham, to sacrifice people to his personal and professional needs. Williams admits that his "ratio of concerns" puts friendship well below his work and his hypochondria, but protests that, despite being "fantastically self-centered," he is not a disloyal friend; there is not much evidence here to support that contention. Margo Jones, so instrumental in getting Williams' early work produced, is scrapped from *You Touched Me!* after doing the play in Pasadena ("Margo will not be crushed over being left out of a possible Broadway production. I told her right along that she would have to take her chances on that and she knows it"). And after a rare act of loyalty, when he insists on signing his friend Mary Hunter to direct the play in New York over the objections of his agent, he cans her the moment Guthrie McClintic shows some interest ("Naturally I'm sorry for her . . . but no reasonable person would act otherwise. . . . And after all, McClintic!").

Of course, the annals of Broadway are bursting with such stories, and, besides, we expect an artist to be ruthless on behalf of his art. Too often, however, Williams seems ruthless on behalf of his career. His friend Windham quotes from an interview Williams once gave to the *Times* in which he said: "The real fact is that no one means a great deal to me, anyway . . . I prefer people who can help me in some way or other, and most of my friendships are accidental." Windham adds: "I had a hard time convincing outraged acquaintances that he was saying no one meant a great deal to him compared to his work, that he preferred people whose private responses helped him with this private vocation." The tone is exculpatory and sympathetic, but if one listens carefully, one can just hear the shrill whistle of a long-suppressed rage. Donald Windham has published a very damaging book, in which a man who tended to treat people as objects becomes something of an object himself. And thus, the whirligig of time brings in his revenges.

(1978)

PART II

FISCAL MOMENTS:
Funding for the Arts

CONTENTS

ONE

Art Versus Advocacy

FOR FOUR DAYS in June 1976, Yale University played host to the artistic directors, managing directors, board members, and other delegates of over a hundred nonprofit professional American theatres in a conference designed to air their mutual problems and concerns. By the time the conference was over, identifying the precise nature of these problems and concerns had become a source of considerable disagreement.

I was present to report the event for this article, although I also served as a participant and panelist in my capacity as director of the Yale Repertory Theatre, and as a representative of the host institution. But aside from providing the seat and facilities for the conference, Yale played a rather peripheral role. Sponsored by the Theatre Communications Group—a national agency established in 1961 to provide a variety of services to eligible theatrical institutions—the conference was actually the brainchild of TCG's taciturn director, Peter Zeisler, who originally conceived of it as a purified version of the First Annual Congress on Theatre (FACT), held on the

Princeton campus two years ago. Whereas FACT was ecumenical in spirit, an attempt to weld an alliance between the commercial stage and the resident theatre movement for mutual advantage, the TCG conference was more exclusive in conception, open only to nonprofit theatres, and looking for union not with Broadway but with other subsidized arts institutions, such as symphony orchestras, opera and ballet, and museums. What both conferences shared, aside from the occasional tempests ruffling their placid Ivy League settings, was an almost obsessive preoccupation with money.

This was probably related to what Mr. Zeisler calls "the extraordinary diversity and growth of the nonprofit professional theatre since the early sixties" because the proliferation of these institutions was such that their activities were beginning to outstrip their subsidies. It was time, the TCG board believed, for an advocacy program designed "to change perceptions nationally about our theatres" so that the federal government, the private foundations, and corporations might increase their contributions. Indeed, raising public consciousness was the subject of the keynote address, delivered at a Sunday banquet in Woolsey Hall after President Kingman Brewster, Jr., of Yale had welcomed the participants. The speaker was W. McNeil Lowry, former vice president of the Ford Foundation and *éminence grise* of the resident theatre movement by virtue of being the first to give it substantial financial and moral support.

Addressing a group that included, among representatives of theatres large and small, such luminaries as Gordon Davidson of the Mark Taper Forum, Zelda Fichandler of the Arena Stage, Jose Delgado of El Teatro Campesino, Lloyd Richards of the O'Neill Theatre Center, T. Edward Hambleton of the Phoenix Theatre, John Houseman of the Acting Company, Bernard Gersten of the Public Theatre, Marshall Mason of the Circle Repertory Company, and Robert Kalfin of the Chelsea Theatre. Mr. Lowry advised the conference that the central question was not "how much money for the arts, but why money for the arts in the first place." He called, in other words, for the definition of a public policy that would establish artistic activity as important in itself, and not just as a useful extension of the educational process or social uplift. Attempting to set some guidelines for this policy, Mr. Lowry urged that professional performance be strictly distinguished from amateur performance, that quality provide the prime standard of value in determining support, and that Broadway and the nonprofit theatres maintain a wary distance from each other ("Already there are worrying signs that nonprofit theatres moving into Broadway productions may risk losing artistic control of repertory; it is very difficult to be just half commercial.") Speaking in dry, muted tones to the opening assembly, Mr. Lowry concluded his remarks with a warning—"it is easier to popularize the arts away than to repress them"—that was probably the most provocative thing said at the conference, considering the implications for any honest arts advocacy program in a utilitarian society dominated by consensus thinking.

But Mr. Lowry's words were to go largely unheeded in the speeches and panels that followed, where the "why" was often eclipsed by the "how" and where discriminations of quality tended to get blurred either by harmonizing sentiments or by ideological tub thumping. Nancy Hanks, for example, the gracious head of the National Endowment for the Arts, called for a power network which would include *all* forms of theatre, whether nonprofit, commercial, academic, or amateur, while John O'Neal of the Free Southern Theatre seemed more concerned with separatism, chiding the conferees for producing "irrelevant" classics while "the people" were living in poverty, and dedicating his own work to "the struggle for liberation of the black nation" from the "oppressor." Other uses of the theatre were described in panels devoted to outreach programs ("Moving the Mountain to Mohammed") and to minority companies ("The Third World Continuum") where participants validated their work as a way of reaching ghetto children, raising sensitivity, or "turning on young people to their own creativity."

Mr. Lowry's concern for artistic quality was generally disregarded in the larger meetings as well, which seemed more preoccupied with the mechanics of audience building, influencing the political structure, and image-making. While a few panels were devoted to such aesthetic issues as the relationship of the director to the designer and the use of music in production, most centered on such technical questions as fund-raising methods ("Other Ways of Skinning the Fat Cat"), techniques of increasing subscriptions ("Subscribe Now!"), and establishing local public action networks ("How to Make Your Friends Influence People"). Typical of these was a panel called "Providing Information to and from Congress and Public Agencies," the information providers being two Washington lobbyists who cheerfully explained how their methods might be adapted to arts advocacy. One of these, Frederick J. Weintraub, a lobbyist for the Council for Exceptional Children (a rubric which includes both the gifted and the handicapped), proceeded to give an interesting illustration of how he achieved "the ultimate goal of a lobbyist . . . to be perceived by policy makers as the sole purveyor of truth." First, he ghosted a speech for a friendly congressman on behalf of his client group, providing a questionable statistic for the occasion, and then he cited the statistic as fact in his own propaganda, attributing it to his congressional source: "Basically," he added, "the game you're involved in is creating truth."

This was received by most of the audience with all the awe due someone functioning pragmatically in the real world, and it was not long before other conferees were flinging around statistics and dressing their speech with such epithets as "power understanding." Privately, a few conference members were beginning to express dismay over the growing prevalence of advertising jargon and public relations euphemisms among people presumably working in an art form, and this was dramatized when a small controversy arose, during a panel on

"The Printed Word," over whether theatre publications should be used to disseminate helpful "information" about the nonprofit theatres or for the purpose of disinterested criticism. It was soon apparent that rigorous criticism, however sympathetic, was not very welcome at many theatres represented; and while the word "publicity" was never mentioned, it was clear from the discussion that the printed word was generally respected only as a medium for institutional boosterism.

Those who like myself had come to the conference prepared to discuss artistic issues were rapidly learning that its real subject was image-building. As a result, I helped to launch another controversy when one of the few panels devoted to an aesthetic question—"Defining the Statement a Theatre Makes"—was abruptly canceled by the TCG board. An informal poll of the conferees, Mr. Zeisler announced, had revealed that most were more interested in pursuing the question of advocacy than in listening to a group of artistic directors (myself among them) define the identity of their theatres, and the schedule was revised accordingly. The unexpected outcry following this decision forced a rescheduling of the artistic directors' panel the next day on a reduced scale, but it helped to articulate some of the apprehensions that were building over the narrowness of the conference, and to locate a fear developing among some conferees, particularly the representatives of the smaller theatres, that they were being manipulated for a prearranged purpose.

Mr. Zeisler took the opportunity to reread his letter of invitation to the assembly, which declared that the conference would center on the "fiscal crisis" and on ways "to investigate and explore our potential for public action." But it seemed to some of us that certain important related questions were not being fully discussed. One had to do with how a theatre can maintain its animating idea at the same time that it perpetuates itself as an institution; another with how a democratic nation can be persuaded to help subsidize an art form which might be subversive of majority opinion; another with what impact a Broadway transfer has on the integrity of a resident theatre (Robert Kalfin testified, movingly, that the worst thing ever to befall the Chelsea was the Broadway success of *Candide*); still another was whether all the theatres represented at the conference deserved to be subsidized in the first place. Discussion of these questions flowed freely in the corridors and anterooms, but although they were raised during the conference itself, they were rarely addressed, much less resolved.

The one question that *was* resolved was the question of advocacy. During the final moments of the conference, a motion was proposed and passed, urging the TCG board, augmented by other theatre representatives, to explore in coordination with other nonprofit organizations how to increase public support for the arts. The perfunctory manner in which this resolution was discussed caused Margot Lewitin of the Interart Theater to protest that the conferees had been railroaded and that advocacy had always been the sole issue of the conference; and it inspired Louis Scheeder of the Folger Theater Group to ask how a service organization like TCG could assume the powers of a political organization without having been elected by a membership. Mr. Zeisler, still taciturn but now rather weary, responded that TCG was not a membership agency and that it was simply trying to represent the wishes of the assembly, while Arvin Brown, director of the Long Wharf Theater and president of TCG's board, deploring the "paranoia" he saw building among the conferees, declared that it was not the advocacy resolution that made the conference memorable, but rather "the tiny moments of coming together."

Not surprisingly, however, it was not harmony and togetherness that were the most vivid impressions at the conference close. It was a moot question whether any organization could effectively unify such disparate theatre groups, but real divisions had nevertheless opened up in the nonprofit movement which did not bode well for the future success of advocacy.

The smaller theatres felt overwhelmed by the larger ones; those with aesthetic goals were being challenged by those with social and political purposes; and, most important to my mind, artistic directions were in danger of being rerouted by managerial concerns.

The foundation executives, board members, producers, and managers who really dominated this meeting were, after all, attempting to bring us to some clear awareness of the practicalities of life—and for a very pressing reason: the survival of our theatres. But aside from the obvious difficulty of bringing a group of scratchy, idiosyncratic individualists into agreement on anything, there was the gnawing question of whether it was possible to coordinate the purpose of art—which has something to do with truth—with the techniques of advocacy—which has mostly to do with appearance. Were the means getting confused with the ends? It was interesting to speculate about what Bernard Shaw or Anton Chekhov might have replied to these questions, and what Henrik Ibsen might have said to a lobbyist who told him, "Basically the game you're involved in is creating truth." But the playwrights hadn't been invited to this conference, and the last thing most people seemed interested in discussing was the relationship of their theatres to the art they presumably embodied and served.

(1976)

TWO

Can the Show Go On?

HERE ARE a few of the things that happened to performing arts institutions between July 1976 and July 1977:

· The Joffrey Ballet canceled its entire spring season.
· The New York City Ballet was shut down by a musicians' strike.
· The American Shakespeare Festival in Stratford, Conn., failed to open for its 1977 season, and its future is in doubt.
· The American Ballet Theatre averted bankruptcy by selling its Chagall sets.
· The Saratoga Performing Arts Center cut back its orchestra season by one-quarter.
· The Buffalo Philharmonic spent $900,000 of its endowment to pay pressing debts.
· The Hartford Ballet reduced its touring season from twenty-six weeks to six weeks.
· The Metropolitan Opera succeeded in salvaging its 1977

season by raising $12.5 million in emergency funds, and now needs an additional $11 to $14 million annually merely to open.

• Joseph Papp announced his decision to withdraw from Lincoln Center, and to close down all operations of the New York Shakespeare Festival at the Vivian Beaumont.

Is there a crisis in the performing arts? The question is obviously rhetorical, and the various foundation officers, artistic directors, managing directors, board members, advocacy chairmen and agency officials whom I interviewed recently over a period of weeks confirmed an impression that the problem is fast approaching the critical point.

Nobody is in disagreement over the cause: Symphony orchestras, dance and ballet companies, opera companies, and theatres are all experiencing an inflationary increase in expenses accompanied by a corresponding decrease in private giving. As a recent report puts it: "The rise in demand for the arts, and the increasing popularity of the arts, means that arts organizations must provide more services to the community. That in turn means more performers and staff, for arts organizations are 'labor intensive.' " But at the same time that services are multiplying and performing arts groups are proliferating, the gap between income and expenses is steadily widening. (Even though audiences pay as much as $22.50 a ticket at the Metropolitan Opera, they are still being substantially subsidized by the arts institutions.) Most important, the traditional sources of support—particularly the private foundations—are reducing rather than increasing their subsidies.

Take the largest of these, the Ford Foundation, for years the foremost patron of the performing arts in the United States. A shrinking portfolio has reduced Ford's total annual grants by more than half—but its contribution to the arts has been slashed by more than four-fifths! More ominous than these statistics for the future of the arts at the foundation was the tone of Henry Ford's recent letter of resignation from the board of trustees, where he singled out the Office of the Arts as an area which has ceased to be "innovative" and "experimental," instead sticking "with some programs for years and years." Mr. Ford was critical not only of the foundation's continuing support for existing programs, but of its failure to appreciate "private enterprise" and reward "individual" achievement—hardly cheering to the performing arts which, by their very nature, are essentially collective, cooperative, and collaborative public structures.

When I interviewed McGeorge Bundy, president of the Ford Foundation, in the company of his newly appointed "acting" vice president for the arts, Roger Kennedy, it was clear that the foundation was in the throes of change. Large numbers of staff had recently been "terminated," and Mr. Bundy was preparing to rent the empty offices of this resplendent glass building to outside tenants. While assuring me of his ongoing commitment to the arts, Mr. Bundy was equally firm in expressing his conviction that "the foundations are not the solution." The appointment of Mr. Kennedy, whom I knew only as a fiscal officer of the foundation, to reexamine the Ford's arts policy was a signal that some sort of radical cutback was under way, and the figures I received confirmed this melancholy supposition. The foundation's arts commitment used to be $20 million annually. It is now down to $4 million, with $1.4 million of the total going to nonprofit film distribution. Mr. Bundy dismissed my conjecture that Henry Ford's admiration for individual rather than institutional achievement was having any influence on foundation policy. But with reductions of this kind, it was inevitable that grants to individual artists would begin to eclipse assistance to institutions. Such giving is both cheaper and more visible than the kind of support Ford was once able to provide, when it lavished $80 million on symphony orchestras and $25 million on resident theatre companies.

The Rockefeller Foundation—formerly second only to Ford in its annual support for the performing arts—has already begun pursuing a policy of small grants to the "creative person," with only token help going to the institutions that support such persons. In theatre, for example, Rockefeller makes about eight annual grants of $8,500 to playwrights, along with $3,000 to the theatres with which the playwrights ask to be associated. Rockefeller's arts director, Howard Klein, told me that his foundation is in no position to respond to cries for help from ailing institutions. The main criterion for its "programatic" grants, he said, is "quality," though he conceded that his staff was too small to make many qualitative judgments. Thus, Klein turned down a survival appeal from the trouble-ridden American Shakespeare Festival, even though he had never seen a play there—his decision was partially based on "reading the reviews over the years." An equally compelling reason, one suspects, was budgetary: Rockefeller, which gave almost $3.5 million to 47 performing arts institutions in 1972 gave, in 1976, only $2 million to 30 such institutions, with $1.4 million of the total going to a program invented and entirely funded by the foundation—New World Records, Inc., which manufactures albums of American music. This leaves $600,000 annually for all the live performing arts, a precipitous drop of nearly 85 percent in four years!

Other private foundations, like the Andrew Mellon and the Shubert, are still strongly committed to the performing arts, but their policies or portfolios are not sufficient to generate more than occasional relief. Mellon, under its young arts administrator, David Saltonstall, normally changes its beneficiaries from year to year to accommodate larger three-year grants to different kinds of institutions—resident theatres in 1974, modern dance companies in 1975, classical ballet in 1976, symphony orchestras in 1977 (Mr. Saltonstall would like to repeat the cycle when these grants run out). As for Shubert, this foundation has mainly been supporting theatres, preferably (though not exclusively) those which "stimulate the economy" by developing plays for New York. I found a general apprehension among some foundation officers that Ford or

Rockefeller would disburden themselves of responsibility for the arts in the belief that other philanthropies were picking up the tab. But virtually all these officers were agreed that federal, state, and corporate money was the only answer to declining private support.

Of all these money sources, the corporate role is at once the most promising and the most problematical, depending on whom you talk to. Goldwin A. McLellan, president of the Business Committee for the Arts, holds the unshakable conviction that "there are only two areas that will solve the crisis for the arts—the business community and private philanthropists." This view is warmly seconded by his vice president, Gideon Chagy, who, upon my arrival at BCA, uncorked the stunning news that corporate support for the arts in 1976 (admittedly the Bicentennial year) amounted to $221 million, or almost two and a half times the total budget of the National Endowment for the Arts. Where is all this money going? Doubtless corporate philanthropy is often imaginative and altruistic, but a disproportionate share of these tax-free contributions is being poured into television, still the favorite medium of the "new patrons of the arts" (as Mr. Chagy calls them in a book of that name). While corporations had no trouble underwriting such popular programs as BBC's *Upstairs, Downstairs,* they were much more hesitant about supporting *Visions,* a series of original television plays by new American dramatists—"Business concerns," the New York *Times* reported recently, "were reluctant to be associated with the series because many of its dramas have controversial themes."

Examples like this confirm a suspicion that much corporate support for the arts tends to be a dignified form of institutional advertising, avoiding the hard-sell approach of traditional sponsorship but retaining many of the same prohibitions. As Lincoln Kirstein, general director of the New York City Ballet, puts it wanly, "Big advertisers will not allow you to be left with a vision superior to that of Mobil or Exxon." An official of the National Endowment for the Arts is even more blunt: "Corpo-

rations are buying the arts like they buy any other commodity." Still, things start to get rather fuzzy when you try to
determine exactly which arts are being bought. Mr. McLellan
told me, for example, that seven cents of every corporate arts
dollar (amounting to $15 million, or four times the figure
disbursed by the National Endowment) is going to legitimate
theatres. But he could not immediately identify which theatres
were receiving benefits, aside from those produced on the PBS
Theater in America series and those, like Kennedy Center and
Lincoln Center, receiving aid from the United Corporate
Fund. Finally, he remembered a theatre entirely funded by
corporate money—the La Crosse Community Theatre in La
Crosse, Wisconsin, which was built, maintained, and supported for the creative expression of its employees by the
Trane Corporation, a manufacturer of heating equipment.

Obviously, not everyone would agree that this constitutes a
genuine contribution to theatre—and the problem is even
more widespread. While more Americans than ever believe
the arts to be important to the quality of life (89 percent,
according to a recent Harris poll), there seems to be considerable confusion over precisely what the arts are. "The arts
crisis," according to Marcia Thompson of the Ford Foundation, "is a lack of clear definition of what we are talking about.
There is no national voice of sufficient strength to make
qualitative judgments." There is no strong national policy
either. According to Joan Mondale—President Carter's chief
unofficial spokesman on the subject—the arts are defined by
the yearning of most Americans for "personal expression."
This is warm and democratic, but it does little to distinguish
high art from basket-weaving, or trained horn players from the
brass section of the high school band. As for the National
Endowment for the Arts, this important federal agency is
growing increasingly vague about what areas are meant to lie
within its mandate. One officer there complained to me recently that of the twelve divisions funded by the NEA, only six
could properly be called "arts"—the rest include such mar-

ginal endeavors as folk arts, handicrafts, inner-city community activity, social and ethnic programs and the like.

Problems of definition are only one of the dilemmas afflicting the National Endowment; others may prove even more discouraging to those who pinned their hopes on rescue from the public sector. Federal, state, and municipal contributions to performing arts institutions remain an important component of annual budgets, but the money is not increasing fast enough; it is being spread too thin and in some cases it is compounding existing problems. The New York State Council on the Arts is both generous and discriminating in its support of the performing arts, but in this it is virtually unique; most city and state arts agencies are too small to provide more than moral support. And while the National Endowment can proudly point to annual increases in appropriations from Congress, after twelve years it still has not reached the $100-million mark, and the United States continues to lag behind every other major country, including Canada, in per-capita contributions to the arts. Moreover, legislative pressure to distribute grants on a geographic basis, regardless of quality or number (Shubert's Gerald Schoenfeld calls this "force-feeding the boondocks"), is having a starvation effect on some of the major urban performing arts centers. No theatre company, for example, receives more than $150,000 annually from the National Endowment, though some of the budgets are in the millions, and even the Endowment's 1976 grant of $600,-000 to the Metropolitan Opera represented only 2.4 percent of the Met's annual expenditure of $25 million.

An added difficulty—the consequences of which have yet to be measured—is being created by a new National Endowment program—the challenge grant, whereby eligible institutions receive $1 in federal funds for every $3 they can raise from the community. Matching grants of this kind are designed to stretch the fund-raising capacities of performing arts organizations, to increase fiscal responsibility, and to stimulate independent private support—all laudable goals. But whatever the financial benefits that may accrue from this plan, the challenge grant is virtually guaranteed to reward sophisticated managements at the expense of less well-administered groups, meanwhile encouraging everyone to become more expert at producing money than at producing works of art. Those organizations without their own fund-raisers will be forced to hire some for the purpose, thus inflating the budget that has to be raised by swelling the already large managerial bureaucracy—an example of the way federal money can sometimes exacerbate the condition it is trying to cure.

Another example is the growing list of rules and regulations to which each institution must conform in order to receive federal money. Typical of these is Section 504 of the Rehabilitation Act, prohibiting discrimination against the physically and mentally handicapped (alcoholics and drug addicts included) in federally assisted programs. One of the features of this otherwise compassionate piece of legislation may have dire effects on the arts—the requirement that every performance area be "barrier-free" within three years so as to provide easy accessibility to people in wheelchairs, as well as to provide aids to the deaf and the blind. The cost of such structural alterations—new ramps, elevators, audio equipment, expanded lavatories, etc.—is estimated in the billions. And although the federal government may provide some of the money needed to alter these spaces, there is little doubt that such additional funds will also be counted as "aid to the arts," taking the place of incremental support for basic programs.

In short, like the private educational institutions, the performing arts organizations are learning that federal money has restrictions as well as advantages. And while the government's insistence on compliance with social-action programs is undoubtedly preferable to its previous pressure for conformity in the political area, the consequences may be just as limiting to the artist. One cannot escape the conclusion that the major sources of financial support, which spell the difference between survival and extinction, are either in the process of

drying up or are proving insufficient. The result: The performing arts are destined to undergo a profound change.

One inevitable consequence is that a number of American
companies will soon be closing down. Almost all of the people
I talked to expect a serious depletion in the ranks of symphony
orchestras, opera companies, resident theatres, dance companies, and ballet groups over the next few years. True, there
was a general consensus that the large establishment institutions—the "dinosaurs," as one person called them—would
survive the crisis, since their demise would have a serious
effect on American prestige abroad. But even here, there was
not total confidence. McGeorge Bundy, for example, though
"betting against the death of any large institution," speculated
that the Metropolitan Opera might call a "sabbatical—it might
go dark for a year," while Amyas Ames, chairman of Lincoln
Center, could not assure me that the Met would be able to
open after the coming season. Regardless of how they viewed
the Met, almost everyone agreed that the smaller, more mar-
ginal institutions would expire without an extraordinary emer-
gency plan; and Mr. Bundy believed that the New York City
Ballet might be among those going down.

An equally important worry is whether survival would be
worth it, given the kinds of changes these institutions are
being forced to make in order to stay alive. One obvious transformation now overtaking the performing arts is the subordi-
nation of their artistic growth to managerial know-how. Partly
in response to foundation pressure for more "fiscal credibility," many arts organizations are at present being run by their
administrators, if not by their boards, with much time and
energy being expended on behalf of new membership techniques, marketing, audience development, and increased royalties. These administrators now hold the power to hire and
fire the artistic director, largely on the basis of his capacity to
deliver audiences or develop income-producing properties;
no wonder the work is becoming increasingly commercial. The
most obvious victims of this change in structure are the resi-

dent theatres. Many are establishing close ties with the commercial theatre network, and—sometimes in partnership with a Broadway producer—are selecting plays and developing productions that can be moved intact to New York.

Some observers consider this a subsidized form of out-of-town tryouts, the resident theatre taking over the role previously performed by the Shubert chain. Others, notably Gerald Schoenfeld of the Shubert organization, are more sanguine about this development, considering it both financially shrewd and culturally inevitable: "Broadway is merely a geographical location. Broadway theatre is no more commercial than most large regional theatres. We deal with the same union, we suffer from the same economic problems, we attract the same audience, we charge the same prices, we strive for the same standard of excellence. The only differences are we pay taxes and we receive no subsidy. In a capitalistic society like ours, paying taxes is a noble pursuit." The observation is true, though it is sad that so few find it regrettable. Actually, the Kennedy Center is virtually indistinguishable, in its theatrical activities, from a commercial management, even though it was constructed with the aid of $43 million in federal funds and is soon to receive $4.5 million more for repairs. It is no wonder that some Broadway producers, like Richard Barr, president of the League of New York Theatres, are beginning to demand government subsidy for commercial theatre. Some of the subsidized theatres now resemble Broadway in everything but name.

And this condition is not exclusive with the theatre. The Metropolitan Opera recently created a partnership with the Kennedy Center, for the purpose of booking attractions during the off-season—Olivia Newton-John, the pop singer, has just finished such an engagement at the Met. "Isn't the Met commercial?" reasons Mr. Schoenfeld. "They have a restaurant, a bookstore. Isn't the Smithsonian commercial? They have a garage business, a book business, a souvenir business, they rent cassettes. We don't have fully subsidized theatre in

America. What we have is a little government funding, some private support—and the rest is business."

Of course, his point is indisputable. And it is as a business —as a "major growth industry," in fact—that lobbying groups and advocacy committees feel compelled to "sell" the arts nowadays. The publications of the National Endowment proudly observe that "though the arts are not self-supporting, they are a fertile economic resource, generating over $3 billion in expenditures and receipts annually." And the National Report on the Arts, a publication sponsored by Amyas Ames's National Committee for Cultural Resources, makes its appeal not so much on the basis of aesthetic achievement as on the synergistic influence the arts are having on the economy—the jobs created, the tourists attracted, the restaurants and hotels filled, the goods and services purchased: "Arts organizations," the report concludes, "play a vigorous, stabilizing, even vital role in the economic life of the nation and of its states and cities." This makes good, sound, practical sense, all right. But it might have given some American performing artists pause, when they were first practicing an instrument or learning a plié, to know that their work would have to be justified on the basis of how it helped to stimulate the economy or how it helped sell T-shirts or posters in the lobby during intermission.

As a matter of fact, the general effect of all this on the American performing artists has been far from salutary. Alwin Nikolais the choreographer is only one of those to express despair lately over how much time must be spent in filling out quadruplicate application forms for funds, while Alvin Ailey, both exhausted and depressed, is preparing to take a year off from his company, finding that the demand on him for fund-raising, for "hobnobbing with politicians and kissing so-and-so's hand at a cocktail party," is cutting seriously into his creative life: "Man, that's like seven hours of rehearsal. I could have made a new dance in that time." As for the Paul Taylor dance group, having run out of funds, it had to abandon last season's appearance at the City Center: "Tomorrow," a New York *Post* item announces, "the dancers are staging a picnic at City Center, where industrialists and other potential sponsors will be wooed with wine, dance and food."

When do performing artists prove their quality enough to stop rattling the tin cup? Apparently never. Joseph Papp finds this both outrageous and humiliating: "It's downhill all the way. It's disgraceful for us, and even the Met, to have to go begging for money. It's not just the indignity of raising cash all the time. It's ridiculous. It doesn't work."

But Lincoln Kirstein's long experience with the New York City Ballet and School of American Ballet has taught him that the situation is chronic: "I have come to the conclusion," he told me recently, "that it isn't going to improve because the performing arts are neither a necessity nor a service. The biomorphic unit, the biped man, doesn't change—for a long time he has lived by bread alone. There's no Eleventh Commandment that says, Thou shalt have symphony orchestras." Kirstein believes that most people are terrified of the imaginative process, and don't like to talk about quality because they don't know how to measure it. "Only a very small elite feel that art is a necessity. The rest treat it as a diversion. A diversion from what? General horror and boredom."

Many years in the lists have taught Kirstein to be philosophical. The scrappy Joe Papp, on the other hand, has been impelled by his fiscal troubles into new heights of combativeness. "I want the arts to be considered part of the national crisis and not just our own crisis," he says. "The time is over to depend on private support. The question is, Do you want us or not?" Papp has found it impossible to operate the Vivian Beaumont under present conditions. He receives $175,000 annually from the United Corporate Fund, and about a half-million dollars more from miscellaneous foundations, but he has had to pay Lincoln Center $450,000 each year just for housekeeping expenses (the Met pays out $3 million for the same services). On a $5-million budget at the Beaumont, Papp estimates that within two years Lincoln Center would have drained all his money, including his profits from *A Chorus Line.*

Papp is convinced that the only answer to his and others' problems lies in massive infusions of federal funds—sums not just in the millions but in the billions. And in this, President Carter will have to play a crucial role. "In the same way he's conserving fuel, he must conserve these resources. We are part of the crisis—a multimillion crisis area. You have to up the stakes. The ante must be raised." When I ask him how he would persuade a populist President, even one who listens to Mozart while he works, to support such a relatively elitist enterprise as the performing arts, Papp proposed his dramatic gesture: "I'm going to abandon my operation at the Beaumont, and I wouldn't be surprised if some of the other performing arts institutions join me. Imagine what this country would be like without its cultural institutions. Let Lincoln Center become a burnt-out area like the South Bronx—let graffiti be the only trace of art in those buildings."

Whether the other institutions elect voluntarily to close down with Papp by means of a general strike, or as seems more likely, to close involuntarily because of a failure to meet expenses, the nature of the crisis is becoming clear. For all the interest in the arts today, no clear authoritative voice is doing the work of judgment and definition. And without a national conscience to prod and protect them, the performing arts are being caught in a crunch among three strong forces—American individualism, American utilitarianism, and American capitalism—all of them considerably more powerful than the appetite for creative fulfillment. Individualism, if sympathetic at all to the arts, is more responsive to stars and soloists and personalities than to institutions, perhaps oblivious to the fact that playwrights cannot function without theatres any more than violinists can play without orchestras or prima ballerinas can dance without ballet companies. Utilitarianism, accustomed to measuring things with practical yardsticks, is unable to comprehend the invisible values of art. And capitalism distrusts all systems that fail to return tangible rewards or to prove themselves in the marketplace. As a result, private enterprise is gradually crushing the delicate quasi-socialist membrane of the communal performing arts, or is changing them into something more commensurate with traditional commercial values.

Well, private enterprise has certainly made its contributions to our national life, but it hasn't done very well by our cities or our natural environment, and it's not likely to do much more for our music, dance, or theatre. What is obviously required now is for the federal government to recognize that the performing arts are an endangered natural resource, worthy of preservation like other treasures of nature, and like them, in serious jeopardy of being polluted by commercial wastes. After all, one doesn't measure the value of the Colorado River or the Teton Mountains by how many tourists they attract or how many hot-dog stands they support; by the same reasoning, the arts must not be subject to economic or numerical criteria.

They are nourishment for the soul and, as Bernard Shaw observed in a passage I like to quote, the soul is a very expensive thing to feed: "It eats music and pictures and books and mountains and lakes and beautiful things to wear and nice people to be with. In this country you can't have them without lots of money; that is why our souls are so horribly starved." In our own soul-starved country, we can't have such things without lots of money either. But if we lose the performing arts, after this long, difficult struggle to create and sustain them, then the blight on our spirits will be irreversible and profound.

(1977)

THREE

The Future of the Endowments

I MADE a journey to Washington in the fall of 1977 armed only with a notebook and an overnight bag, to learn more about the federal government's relationship to the arts and humanities in America. Created under the National Foundation on the Arts and Humanities Act of 1965, and amended and extended under the Arts, Humanities and Cultural Affairs Act of 1975, the twin Endowments—the National Endowment for the Humanities and the National Endowment for the Arts—are now in their twelfth year of operation, with a total appropriation of $225 million (including $36 million in challenge grants). Both have recently received new leadership—appointments that are attracting considerable criticism. And so I was eager to discover, through interviews with various movers and shakers on the Hill, in what directions the Endowments were preparing to move under the Carter administration.

My curiosity was not entirely disinterested. Along with most other resident and experimental theatres, the Yale Repertory Theatre receives a crucial, though still insufficient, annual grant from the National Endowment for the Arts, while the National Endowment for the Humanities, until very recently, helped to support the criticism and dramaturgy program at the Yale School of Drama. My experience as a panel member with both Endowments in the past had introduced me to the procedures and personnel of the previous administrations; now I had the opportunity to use this background, as well as my background in the arts, in pointed questioning of the politicians and officers responsible for any new Endowment policies. For one relatively inexperienced about the inner workings of government, this visit was a revelation, one that left me a little shaken about the future of the Endowments and their capacity to withstand internal and external pressure.

I arrived on a brilliant fall Sunday. The sun, glancing off the roofs and domes of the gleaming white government buildings, highlighted both the beauty and the formality of the Capitol, as well as dramatizing a certain quality of artifice. My first meeting was over breakfast at my hotel with Joseph D. Duffey, the newly appointed chairman of the National Endowment for the Humanities. I had known the Reverend Duffey (never intimately) in three capacities: as Democratic candidate for senator from Connecticut in 1970, when he lost to Lowell Weicker; as Cultural Affairs Officer for the State Department; and now as Ronald Berman's successor at the Endowment. I had always found him a gentle and courteous individual, somewhat retiring, but with a particularly agreeable smile.

Duffey looked affable and healthy when I met him this time, though a certain air of melancholy, almost a wistfulness, surrounded his person. He had not sought this position, he told me, but he was excited by its potentiality and eager to embrace his responsibilities. Duffey's appointment had been severely criticized in some quarters, most vocally by Michael Straight, former acting chairman of the National Endowment for the Arts, who, in a sweeping attack on the way the new heads were chosen, charged that Duffey's "primary qualifications are political. He has no credentials in the academic world; his credentials are that when he ran for the senate in Connecticut, he came out for Carter.''

A native of West Virginia with an advanced degree from Yale, Duffey seemed eager to correct the impression (held by some academics as well) that he was not sufficiently qualified for his new job. He had obviously been thinking a lot about the humanities lately. His first task, I thought, was to define them.

This did not prove easy, since Duffey seemed reluctant to identify himself with any fixed principle or position. Like virtually all of the officials I spoke to in Washington, he was anxious to navigate the treacherous waters between "elitism" and "populism," which also meant meditating the factional arguments between the specialists and the generalists. In his opening statement during his nomination hearings, Duffey repeatedly stressed his desire to satisfy all humanistic constituencies and requirements: "There need be no opposition," he said, "between the highest achievements of scholars in the humanities and the conversation of the general public about those things that are meaningful and valuable. . . . There need be no issue of a separated elite as against popular participation. . . . The answer to these issues is: BOTH."

Duffey provided me with an example from his own personal life. He confessed that he had been rather ashamed of his rough West Virginia origins until asked by some Yale students to give a seminar on Appalachia; this taught him that the humanities had reference to cultural experience as well as to scholarship. "I recognize there are certain key disciplines," he added, "but I am really talking about a dimension of learning. The problem in Vietnam was the absolute lack of understanding of the history and culture of another country." Duffey leaned back in his chair, and toyed with his unfinished coffee. "The humanities are history, literature, and language; the goals are understanding rather than problem solving, and a concern with vitality and verve."

There were two continuing, not altogether reconcilable themes threading through Duffey's affirmation: a genuine concern for quality and an equally genuine concern for social utility. The word "excellence" frequently entered his speech, but he hesitated to identify any "national criteria" for excellence. Declaring that "we are trying to encourage, recognize, and acknowledge excellence as a government," Duffey also expressed his suspiciousness of "all people who close quickly on a recognition of excellence." If this sounds like a contradiction, then it was one that served his desire to "respect the worth and taste of people in every section of the country." A high-sounding aim, and a warmly democratic one, but how do you achieve it without jettisoning standards and falling into a flabby populism? Duffey's reply was emphatic: "I've never heard President Carter use the word 'popularization.' You can make something accessible, but you can't make it popular."

Making the humanities accessible was the way he could demonstrate their social utility; this struck me as Duffey's chief enthusiasm. His means were twofold: advocacy and dissemination. Advocacy was to be achieved through vigorous promotion devices ("The future of the humanities," he said, "and public support for them is going to depend on the understanding of the public"). And dissemination was to be practiced through the communications media ("My foremost concern," he told the Senate Committee on Human Resources, "will be to increase access to the manifold riches of the humanities").

What this meant, inevitably, was more attention to the "miracle" of television. Like most Washington administrators, Duffey considers the proudest achievement of the Humanities Endowment under Ronald Berman to be not the development of a new idea or book or work of scholarly research, but rather its support of the Public Broadcasting Service production of *The Adams Chronicles*—"The bringing together," Duffey called it, "of the best scholarly achievements and quality TV production and technology." A more recent source of NEH pride and recipient of its funds is *The Best of Families,* which Duffey described as "a television social history of the period in America between 1880 and 1900, through the eyes of three immigrant families, which reconstructs what life was like then as accurately as we can." When I expressed doubt over whether television dramas, no matter how well-produced or historically accurate, were the best possible examples of humanistic activity, Duffey replied that "a tradition of excellence in public TV is not a bad thing for a culture to try to achieve."

Obviously, television is attractive not only because it makes the humanities accessible, but also because it makes the Humanities Endowment visible. And visibility for this agency has often been a sensitive area of congressional debate. Duffey's predecessor, Ronald Berman, for example, frequently found himself defending his Endowment against the charge (delivered by his adversary, Senator Claiborne Pell) that it lacked a "high recognition factor" in comparison with the Arts Endowment. His answer was instructive: "I think that the humanities in this country tend on the whole not to be the kind of enterprise which is attractive for immediate media coverage. . . . There is an element of privacy in the humanities just as there is an element of familiarity and sometimes notoriety in the arts." Nevertheless, Berman sank $2.5 million into *The Adams Chronicles,* besides initiating support for *The Best of Families.* I had the impression that Duffey, either through political pressure or personal inclination, was planning to place even more emphasis than Berman on televised adaptations of political and social history for the sake of "increasing access to the manifold riches of the humanities."

I asked Mr. Duffey to imagine Edward Gibbon living today and spending sixteen years writing his monumental six-volume *Decline and Fall of the Roman Empire,* only to discover that the major share of state patronage was going not to support him in his labors, but rather to help underwrite a television adaptation of his work, starring Peter Ustinov as Nero and Kirk Douglas as Spartacus. Duffey smiled for a moment, then hastened to assure me that genuine humanistic learning, such as Gibbon's research, would also be served by the Endowment: "Even the highly specialized scholarship in the humanities which carries the risk of pedantry and failure is in the national interest." Clearly, the new chairman of the National Endowment for the Humanities was eager to identify value along the whole spectrum of humanistic endeavor, whether academic or popular, scholarly or general; my major concern was how he was going to identify funds for all of this as well, given the limited amount of appropriations under his discretion. When money is short, distinctions must be made; but I came away from this interview suspecting that, in Duffey's opinion, nothing human was alien to the Humanities Endowment.

Duffey accompanied me outside, where he helped me hail a cab for the Hill. As I rode to my next appointment in the Dirksen Senate Office Building, I watched him, a faint half-smile upon his face, stride along Pennsylvania Avenue—a decent man, afloat on good intentions, already shipping water from the shoals of the political process.

LIVINGSTON BIDDLE had not yet been named chairman of the National Endowment for the Arts when I met with him; instead, he held the title of staff director of the Senate Subcommittee on Education, Arts, and the Humanities. At the time, however, he was the man most frequently mentioned as Nancy Hanks's successor, and he was frank enough to admit that he very much desired the job.

An ingratiating man with a dapper mustache, mutton chops, and graying hair that probably once was red, "Liv" Biddle has had cultural experience as board chairman of the Pennsylvania Ballet Company, chairman of the Division of the Arts at Fordham University, and occasional novelist; and political experience as special assistant to Claiborne Pell, his mentor and friend. In the cafeteria where we spoke (his own office was too small), Biddle outlined the major problems he foresaw facing the arts today.

"The arts in some areas," he told me, "are tending toward a kind of polarization. There are those who believe in strengthening the base of major institutions and those who believe that the arts should be disseminated, so as to reach out to the widest possible audience. This has resulted in a simplistic division between elitism and populism." Like Duffey, Biddle was eager to satisfy both constituencies by finding a "balanced equation" that might unify the warring factions and demonstrate that each was of fundamental importance to the other. When I asked him for an example of this factionalism, he mentioned the struggle—which he felt the National Endowment for the Arts was obliged to mediate in future—between the artist and the teacher of art.

Under Nancy Hanks and her predecessors, the Endowment had generally favored the artist and ignored the educator, but, Biddle said, the Congress was now being subjected to considerable pressure by such educational organizations as the Music Teachers Association and the American Theatre Association to support their applications for NEA funds. When pressed, Biddle admitted that he thought the artist could usually teach his subject better than the educator, but it was obvious that Biddle was going to prove much more responsive to appeals for arts education than previous NEA chairmen. His experience at Fordham had convinced him that the arts can contribute to education, that they are as important to children as reading, writing, and arithmetic.

The conflict he described between art and education struck me as having clear parallels with the division described by Duffey between works of humanistic scholarship and their television versions. In each case, there was competition between those who generated thought or art, and those who disseminated the product to the widest possible audience. (Another point of tension was the division between the professional artist or humanist and the weekend dabbler.) My questions to Biddle were, Who do you favor in this conflict? and How do you satisfy both sides?

Biddle was unwilling to take a side in his conversation with me, or even to admit that the conflict was irreconcilable. It was his belief that the "arts community" (in which he included both artists and teachers) would sooner or later unite, and that a "higher tide" would eventually "life the whole endeavor." When I asked him how he expected to achieve this desired "unity" when the federal money pot was so small, and so many were competing for the same limited funds, he began speaking about the political process in much the same way that Duffey has spoken of "advocacy."

"If the arts are to prosper and flourish," he told me, "their message has to get out to the country." The Arts Endowment, he emphasized, is supported by senators and congressmen and "the voice of the constituent is the one most clearly heard by Congress." Biddle seemed relatively sanguine about receiving assistance in this effort from the Carter administration. As one who helped write the legislation that set up the Endowments, he felt that "talk about the arts on Capitol Hill has more of a ring of authenticity and respectability now than it did in 1965 when some congressmen confused artists with 'belly dancers.' " Although there are still a handful who say that "if the arts can't hack it by themselves, they shouldn't be supported," the arts now engender a level of real enthusiasm, and have collected a number of influential leaders who consider them a real priority—among these, Biddle mentioned Claiborne Pell, Jacob Javits, Hubert Humphrey, and Harrison Williams in the Senate, and John Brademas, Frank Thompson, Albert Quie, Sidney Yates, and Joe McDade in the House.

It was obvious that Livingston Biddle had deep respect for the political process. He proceeded, in fact, to defend himself against charges of "politicization" not by denying his political interests, but rather by affirming that politics was an honorable activity. (In replying to Michael Straight's accusation that his appointment was a political payoff for being "Senator Pell's old college roommate," he said, "I find 'politics' difficult to give a derogatory meaning to because our whole government is based on the political process as translated through our democracy.") He had prepared a speech, he told me, on

"Power, Politics, and the Arts," and in what I assumed to be a few prepared passages from the address, he offered me some pocket definitions:

"Power is the voice that can come out of a new spirit of unity in the arts."

"Politics is the basic democratic manner in which that power is expressed."

"And the result of the two—the political process—benefits the arts and the artist."

I TOOK MY LEAVE of Mr. Biddle and soon got the opportunity to observe first-hand how this process was allowed to work in the halls of Congress. My impression was that its procedures were subterranean, laborious, labyrinthine, and slow—pretty much, in fact, like the congressional transportation system, a combination of elevators, escalators, and open subways, which I used to make my way to the Rayburn Office Building.

There I hoped to determine for myself whether the optimism of the new Endowment heads was justified, by speaking with some of the more influential figures behind the Arts and Humanities Act.

The first I met with was Frank Thompson, Democratic congressman from New Jersey, whom McGeorge Bundy has called "the most interesting and best-informed person in Congress on the subject of the arts and humanities." A tall, distinguished, gray-haired man with a vibrant, slightly raspy voice (perhaps the result of the Tareyton cigarettes he continually smokes), Thompson helped to introduce the bill that brought the Endowments into being. Sitting in an office decorated with honorary degrees, New Jersey artifacts, and a bust of John F. Kennedy, Thompson expressed to me his conviction that the Arts and Humanities should never have been placed under the same umbrella: "We needed the constituency of the Humanities—more glamorous and acceptable then—to get the less-respected Arts through Congress."

Thompson was very impressed by the performance of the

first head of the Humanities Endowment, Barnaby Keeney, who did a "low-key but superb job." When Nixon replaced Kennedy with his choice, Ronald Berman, there was no great objection, though Berman proved to be more "conservative" than expected. Berman did a good enough job, in Thompson's estimation (he was particularly impressed by *The Adams Chronicles*—"spectacularly well done"), but for some reason, he soon came to "irritate the bejesus out of Claiborne Pell." Thompson stretched his long legs in front of him and puffed on his Tareyton in amusement: "Pell, an elitist, objected to Berman on the grounds that Berman was an elitist." The main issue between them concerned Pell's belief that Berman was failing to give any real authority to the State Humanities Councils, and this feud later resulted in Berman's failure to win enough votes for reconfirmation as chairman.

After a considerable search, Thompson went on, Joe Duffey was confirmed, an acceptable candidate who did not rouse much passion either way. Pell, John Brademas, and Thompson preferred Jim Billington, head of the Woodrow Wilson Center, but Billington was blocked by the White House on the grounds that "he was too Ivy League or Oxford." Others turned the position down. And while there was some grumbling about Duffey in the scholarly community, he proved "acceptable and confirmable" as a compromise candidate.

Thompson was amused by the fact that the arts, once considered rather sleazy by the Congress, were now a source of glamour; this made the Arts Endowment tougher to handle than the Humanities Endowment, since politicians were tempted to use it for their own purposes. The original NEA legislation was specially designed "to keep members of Congress the hell out of it," for fear that they might use the agency as a patronage area for their own protégés. As long as visibility in the arts was low, this plan seemed to work. The council appointments were made with great care, and Roger Stevens, the first chairman, did a "really splendid job." When Nancy Hanks succeeded "this low-key but terribly effective guy," she brought in a "good top staff," and herself proved "bright, able, aggressive."

"Overall," Thompson continued, "Nancy did a splendid job, including a lot of first-rate public relations. She got a lot of visibility for herself. All in all, a first-rate pol." So good, in fact, that the press tends to credit her with the steady increase in appropriations enjoyed by NEA over the years, when it was actually Brademas, Javits, and Thompson himself who worked over the Appropriations committee, and pushed the increases through Congress. "Leonard Garment was terribly effective for the arts in the Nixon years and deserves to be mentioned as well."

Thompson obviously had a genuine feeling for the Endowments. He expressed his support of professional excellence, though he did not consider himself an "elitist." He personally enjoyed jazz, and he had a particular interest in rewriting legislation so that unused railroad depots might be converted, with the aid of federal funds, into cultural and community centers.

MY NEXT VISIT brought me into a more high-pressure area, the Members' Dining Room of the House. There, over a plate of the famous bean soup, I discussed with Fred Richmond of Brooklyn the bill he is trying to introduce that would make it possible for individuals to check off contributions, on their tax return forms, for the arts and humanities. Congressman Richmond is an ebullient, fast-talking, redheaded dynamo—a former fund-raiser for Carnegie Hall—who was perpetually leaping from the table to accost some congressman or -woman, to shake hands, and to trade off something for support of his bill; as a result, he has now collected more than a hundred cosponsors. The most optimistic estimates suggest a potential income of $1.7 billion annually for the arts and humanities if the tax checkoff bill goes through, and so I was surprised to find that some of the more knowledgeable politicians I encountered did not hold out too much hope for its passage, or even that it would make its way successfully through the Ways and Means Committee. It was feared that the Richmond bill, if passed, would open the way for such worthy causes as cancer research to demand a checkoff box on the tax form as well.

I had my own worries about the bill—how the moneys raised were going to be distributed. The plan, as Richmond explained it, was to return the funds to the areas of the donors. In other words, the various state councils would be empowered to distribute funds in the arts and humanities proportionate to the contributions in their various geographical locations. What if a worthy artist or scholar or institution was located in an area where nobody took advantage of the tax checkoff option? Were the arts and humanities to be valued and supported purely on the basis of the local interest in them? Richmond didn't have much time to listen to these questions, and I felt a little sheepish for asking them. A worthy bill was struggling for passage, and at the hearings later that afternoon, I joined those speaking in favor of it.

JOHN BRADEMAS, representative from Indiana and House Majority Whip, is one of those who seem to understand the danger of geographical distribution for the arts and humanities. A trim, well-built, and friendly figure whom I interviewed on the run between his office and the chambers of Congress (he was busy supervising a vote on the D.C. Crime Bill), Brademas told me that the two points of tension he foresaw, in regard to the arts and humanities, were quality and accessibility. He is himself from a state with relatively little in the way of arts, but he perceived a real danger in the practice of spreading money over areas that have not yet produced anything, just in order to satisfy a political constituency.

Brademas seemed to have more questions than answers for me that day; it was clear that he wanted to encourage conversation about certain presuppositions. He began by asking, Why is it proper for the public to support the arts? When I mentioned that this was the sort of question that, after twelve years, one would not expect to be asked, Brademas broke down his general question into a group of specific ones. To what extent is it wise for government to provide basic operating costs rather than money for special projects? What should be the proper mix between support for individuals and support for institutions? What should be federal policy on other arts questions, such as the issue of equity for artists in the tax laws? What should be the role of state and local communities in the decision-making process of the federal agency? How do we encourage state legislatures to stimulate more state money for the arts? And finally, how do we find more ways to spread the arts?

I was a little disheartened by the questions, since they implied that certain fundamental policy decisions had not yet been made at the Endowment. Later, it occurred to me that they had been stimulated by the recent changes in Endowment leadership. Actually, I was learning that no issues are ever finally resolved on Capitol Hill. Just as policy seems to change at the Endowments whenever a new President is elected, so the purpose of the Endowment is shaken with the appointment of each new chairman. I was looking for stability in an area that could not function without the proper mix of understanding, judgment, intelligence, firmness, courage, principle, and clarity, and what I was finding instead was a general well-intentioned amorphousness, where a single, carefully applied pressure could completely alter the shape of things.

MY FINAL appointment of the day took place in one of those pressure points—the office of Claiborne Pell, Democratic senator from Rhode Island, and by all accounts, the most powerful figure in Washington in regard to the arts and humanities. I was surprised, when I arrived, to find Pell accompanied by Livingston Biddle, who greeted me warmly. Pell's greeting was rather less warm. He hadn't been informed of the nature of my business, and when I told him about it, he didn't bother to conceal his impatience. To Biddle's apparent discomfiture, Pell announced to me that he had been "through the same

exercise" too many times lately, and he was getting tired of it.
Rather testily, he told Biddle that "maybe we ought to get a
handout printed up" for people like me. Pell, a sleek, slender,
well-tailored man with wavy gray hair and an Ivy League ac-
cent, looked harried and worn when I met him, and I soon
understood the reason for his irritability. Debate was taking
place on another round of energy bills, which was to proceed
through the night, and the buzzers were calling him to vote
throughout our conversation ("We get summoned by bells,"
he said morosely, "like schoolchildren").

After returning from one of these votes, however, Pell
began to relax, and started discoursing freely on the subject
of the Endowments. It was the Berman issue, and his own part
in it, that seemed to occupy his thoughts; he was obviously still
chafing over the bad press he had received at the time. "A
cabal of people," he told me, "thought I was out to screw
Berman. I was even accused of anti-Semitism. The fact is that,
as everybody knows, I played a crucial role in the creation of
the Endowments. I'd be the last person who would wish to
hurt their quality. It's just that Berman had this laying-on-of-
hands approach to his job. He wanted control of the Humanities money when I believed that at least 20 percent of the
appropriation should be administered through the state councils. You can't concentrate grant awards within a closed circle
of academics and scholars. Providing the states with arts and
humanities money puts them in the mainstream of the political
process. It's too bad that people in these fields have such a bad
opinion of politics; politics is the way our system works."*

*Pell's encounters with Berman during the various hearings make fascinat-
ing reading. His treatment of the former Endowment chairman is always lofty,
sometimes insulting, often inquisitorial. And the issue is almost invariably
Berman's preference for scholars over those outside the academic community,
and his refusal to give much authority to the state councils. "What is the
aversion," Pell asked Berman during the 1975 hearing, "that you have and the
humanities council has against the idea of having elected representatives of
the people, the Government, make these appointments? . . . After all, Congress is a democratic instrument. I believe that Washington should be reflective of the local representatives of the people."

After listening to Pell describe the glories of the political process and the virtues of geographical distribution of Endowment funds, I ventured to ask him a hypothetical question.

"Imagine," I said, "the existence of two city-states in Greece. One is called Athens and the other is called Sparta. One city has produced Plato, Aristotle, Socrates, Aeschylus, Sophocles, Euripides, Aristophanes, Thucydides; the other has produced a succession of military heroes. You are in charge of dispensing money to the arts and humanities throughout Greece. Do you still reward these cities on an equal basis?"

Senator Pell answered quickly. "Of course I do—for in that way, I stimulate the arts and humanities in the city that doesn't have them."

Pell offered me an example of the way he thought the arts and humanities could be brought to "barren" areas. He has a plan called "Great Papers," in which the National Endowment for the Humanities provides funds for conferences to be held in far-off places like Nebraska and Montana. "People—and they wouldn't be academics, they'd be people without formal education—would offer papers on the great books. Imagine these people sitting around a wood-burning stove in a frigid plains area, discussing history or literature. I've been ridiculed for this plan, but nobody yet has been able to convince me it isn't a good one."

I tried, without much success: "It seems to me that, as a politician, you are too preoccupied with the political justification of art and learning, and the way you try to do that is by spreading them throughout the land like jam. As a result, you are giving a lot of thought to how to disseminate ideas to large numbers of people, but you don't seem too interested in how those ideas get formulated in the first place. What you are talking about, finally, is not the humanities, but a government-sponsored form of adult education. You're too involved with how to make knowledge popular, and not enough with how this knowledge is developed. The question that interests me is, What can the Endowment do to help sustain a philosopher while he thinks?''

The buzzer summoned Pell for another vote, and so Biddle undertook to answer for him. "We can use the philosopher's values to enrich the lives of people," he said. "I know Ronald Berman thinks this is just public relations, but I believe it to be the prime function of the Endowments. And this way, we can identify, educate, and develop new philosophers from among the people."

An image sprang into my head of a number of supple, well-developed athletes whose muscles are allowed to atrophy for lack of exercise because the coach, when he is not shaking hands with the spectators in the stands, is thinking up ways to recruit a whole new team.

Pell returned from his vote and began to talk about his own background. "I'm not an artist or a humanist myself, but I'm really interested in the subject matter. Probably because some of my family have been artists, and I minored in the visual arts at college. Frankly, I'm not crazy about abstract art, which is why you don't see any on my walls here. But I don't impose my views over those of the chic 86th Street critics. I do insist, however, that the government has an obligation to provide access for everyone to the arts and humanities. That's why the state councils are so important—fifty state leaders who owe no allegiance to the Arts and Humanities Endowment, getting 20 percent of the pie no matter what they do."

At the sound of another buzzer, I rose to go, and Pell shook my hand. "You're connected to a pretty good institution," he said, alluding to my Yale association. "So are you," I answered, and departed the room.

MY INTERVIEWS were completed, but I had one more visit to make—a ceremonial one. The next morning I took a cab to the Naval Observatory, the official residence of Vice President Mondale and his family. Although he never actually lived in it, Nelson Rockefeller had the Naval Observatory redecorated when he was Vice President, and he sometimes entertained there. It is a handsome three-story building on extensive grounds, with strict security; inside, the public rooms have been decorated very "tastefully," which is to say, they give no evidence of human habitation or personal idiosyncrasy.

I was there to meet with Joan Mondale, generally considered the chief unofficial spokesperson on the arts for the Carter administration; it was my hope that our conversation might give me clues about new federal policies in this area. A gracious, slim, attractive woman, Mrs. Mondale was in the company of her appointments secretary and associate, Mary Ann Tighe, a handsome, well-informed, and intelligent young lady.

Before I could ask my questions, Mrs. Mondale took me on a tour of the American paintings, sculptures, and artifacts on the first floor of the house. She spoke easily and informatively in capsule statements about each work, and was particularly animated when she knew the artist personally or had some interesting anecdote to relate. Aside from the Motherwells, De Koonings, Gottliebs, and other paintings on loan, she had a number of craft works on display as well, including baskets which had been woven for her by Navajo Indians. She was obviously as enthusiastic about native crafts as about fine art. As a matter of fact, she had just returned from a trip to West Virginia, where she visited glass blowers and potters; she was now preparing for a trip to New York, where she planned to talk to dancers.

Mrs. Mondale apparently sees it as her mission to stimulate appreciation throughout the land for arts and crafts, largely by expressing her own boundless enthusiasm for them. She seemed to me most knowledgeable about the visual arts, but she also seems to have an interest in photography, ceramics, basket-weaving, and also in architectural restoration (in common with Congressman Thompson, she loves the idea of reconverting abandoned railroad stations and post offices). Mrs. Mondale spoke with particular passion about rediscovering artworks in the American heartland, such as Leonard Baskin's bas-reliefs of Tennessee Presidents which she came upon during her last visit to that state: "There's so much going on in this country," she told me, wrinkling her nose in a smile. "It's really just neat."

With all respect for her enthusiasm, I was eager to learn from Mrs. Mondale precisely what practical steps the Carter administration was planning to take in order to increase appropriations for the arts. When I asked her this question, her face darkened. "Well, the economy is not doing at all well, you know. President Carter is a fiscal conservative and he is obliged to do something first about the $60 billion deficit we have this year. I think it's a good sign that he didn't cut the NEA, don't you, when he's made cuts in most other programs. Is he interested in the arts? I really think he is. He's been very supportive of me, personally. And although he's a very busy man, he's been to the Kennedy Center a lot. It's just that I don't think he can promise big bold new programs at this time."

When I remarked that the performing arts, for example, were in need of much more help from Carter than visits to the Kennedy Center (many theatres, dance groups, orchestras, and opera companies are in danger of collapse for lack of operating money), Mrs. Mondale looked troubled. "Well," she said, "you've got to remember that most dancers and actors and musicians are white, educated, middle-class people. And you can't help them when there's this big social problem to be solved with the blacks and other minority groups."

I feared that artistic questions were getting confused with social problems. The crisis afflicting the arts is not a matter of color—it is threatening Alvin Ailey's mostly black dance company as much as the mostly white City Center Opera—and it is not essentially a matter of jobs either. But this was not the proper occasion for debate. Instead of pursuing this question, I asked Mrs. Mondale whether she thought President Carter, a religious man, might be brought to recognize that the intangible, spiritual values of the arts are essentially different in kind from the material problems the country faces. She thought this was a good idea.

"You know one way the government can help the artist," she said, "is by reforming the tax laws. That way the artist can get a tax deduction by giving his works to museums, and he can benefit through certain changes in the estate tax laws as well."

Having been present at the hearings on this proposal the previous day (they preceded the hearings on the Richmond bill), I was familiar with the plan. But while sympathetic to equitable tax laws for the artist, I thought that increasing the income of relatively well-off individuals seemed considerably less crucial to American culture than helping to preserve the life of some beleaguered artistic organization in danger of ceasing operation altogether. Instead of answering, Mrs. Mondale rewarded me with her most winning smile.

Mary Ann Tighe suggested, at this point, that many government agencies, besides the Endowment, could be of help to the arts, if approached with the right proposals—the Department of Commerce, for example, has money for certain structural changes in cultural institutions (including new wings for museums and theatres, and swimming pools), provided it could be demonstrated that they help improve the quality of life in the community. I was grateful for this suggestion—not because it was practical (an opera company can hardly pay musicians' salaries with swimming pools), but because it showed an understanding that the problems under discussion were not of the kind that could be effectively solved through arts appreciation.

When I rose to take my leave, Mrs. Mondale showed me the rest of the collection, again lecturing briefly on each painting as we passed. The works were beautifully framed and hung—as professionally as if they were sitting in a museum.

FLYING BACK to my own city on that overcast afternoon, enjoying a misted view of Washington's great monuments and public buildings, I reflected on the Endowments and their increasingly cloudy future. It was true enough, as has been charged, that these agencies were being "politicized," but the politicization went much deeper than the intervention of pressure groups, vested interests, and meddling politicians. It was the very politics of consensus American democracy that was now beginning to influence the policies and appointments of these important federal agencies. Once fully professional and oriented toward the artist and the scholar, the Endowments were now preparing to spread their relatively meager moneys among educationalists, audiences, and amateurs as well, on the essentially political assumption that any resources generated by the people should benefit all the people immediately and simultaneously. Nothing else could account for all the attention now being lavished on such extra-artistic, extra-intellectual concerns as advocacy, arts appreciation, geographical distribution, and dissemination through the media.

I puzzled over why politicians were able to understand the necessity for tax-supported cancer research, even though most Americans, fortunately, do not have cancer, but could not appreciate the need to support art and learning, though most of us are not artists or scholars. True, we are all potentially the beneficiaries of medical research, but it is equally true that we can all potentially benefit from scholarly research, philosophical ideas, and artistic achievement, too. What seems likely now, considering the new consensus policies shaping up at the Endowments, is that the seeds of thought and creation will be allowed to wither away in order to satisfy the aspirations of a larger constituency. Over 140 years ago, in his prophetic book, *Democracy in America,* Alexis de Tocqueville had some ominous forebodings about the fine arts in this country which seem relevant today:

I do not believe that it is a necessary effect of a democratic social condition and of democratic institutions to diminish the number of those who cultivate the fine arts, but these causes exert a powerful influence on the manner in which these arts are cultivated. Many of those who had already contracted a taste for the fine arts are impoverished . . . the number of consumers increases, but opulent and fastidious consumers become scarce. . . . The productions of artists are more numerous, but the merit of each production is diminished. . . . In aristocracies, a few great pictures are produced; in democratic countries a vast number of insignificant ones.

When the twin Endowments were first created, many of us had hopes that America had come of age culturally, that it could support the minority of talent, that the imperatives of artistic and intellectual excellence would no longer be overshadowed by the democratic demands of political necessity. For twelve years, those hopes have been more or less sustained. Whether this condition will continue to prevail is an issue now shrouded in serious doubt and considerable uncertainty.

(1978)

FOUR

The Artist
and the Citizen

THE CURRENT attempt of federal, state, and municipal agencies to define themselves in relation to the arts coincides with an apparently unrelated event: the 150th birthday of a great artist, the Norwegian dramatist Henrik Ibsen.

These two events are separated not only in time, but geographically as well. What can a Scandinavian dramatist, who wrote mostly in the nineteenth century, have to tell us about the experience of being an artist in twentieth-century America? And what can he tell us about the relationship of the secular state—which is organized primarily to help create better material lives for its citizens—to the essentially spiritual question of artistic endeavor and artistic development? What in the world can he have to say to us about the complicated question of funding for the arts through agencies of the government?

Well, I believe this renegade Norwegian is in a position to tell us a great deal, if only because—like most of us today who work in the arts—he was continually forced to appeal to his government for money in support of his endeavors. Ibsen was one of the first to recognize that the state had responsibility not only for what he called "the happiness and welfare of the community," but also for "the development of the nation's life." "States like ours cannot defend themselves by their material prosperity," he wrote. "But states like ours can do so if they fulfill themselves in the service of culture, science, art, and literature." In part because so few statesmen understood the obligation to improve the quality of life through support of the arts, Ibsen always felt alienated from the political sphere. And why? Because "the state still sees in science, in art, and in literature only the decorations, not the pillars and beams of the edifice. I think it is about time this humiliating state of affairs came to an end. The man who does the artistic and intellectual work of a nation has a right to carry his head high. He has a right to protest when he sees that he is offered for his labors only a part of the surplus left over after the material needs of the nation have been satisfied, and only, of course, when there is a surplus."

Now, it is plain that this was written a very long time ago, and things have changed a very great deal in the meantime. Why, the arts and the humanities are so universally recognized and appreciated today that each has its own National Endowment which our statesmen have provided with enough hard cash to run the Pentagon, I am told, for a full eight hours. Obviously the arts hold a very high place in the hearts of our lawmakers, and this would have gratified Ibsen immensely, had he lived today. Imagine the delight with which he would have set aside his work on *Peer Gynt* or *Ghosts* to attack the multiple reams of fascinating application forms required to attract those munificent sums, not to mention the extensive budget sheets, progress reports, and final reports, that make it possible for a theatre to receive enough money from, say, the state of Connecticut to pay a portion of the salary of a single actor, provided that actor is not too particular about the quality of his food or clothing. It is impossible to imagine the joy

with which Ibsen would have suspended his writing or rehearsals in order to take a trip to Washington or Hartford, where
he would be given the privilege of justifying his production of
The Master Builder on the basis of how many people it reached
in the inner city, or how effectively it satisfied the requirements
of affirmative-action programs. My irony is admittedly heavy,
but irony aside, it is perfectly obvious that the relationship
between the artist and the state has not really changed much
since Ibsen's day. What has changed, I believe, is the official
language—the way in which words can be manipulated and
altered to prevent any change. Take the word *art*, for example,
which in the titles of certain federal and state agencies now
seems to be a synonym for sociology, psychological therapy,
social welfare, crafts and hobbies, economic neighborhood
building, racial and ethnic consciousness-raising, aid to the
handicapped, and pork barreling. It is true that the word *art*
has a kind of magical power today; it is also true that the word
is so imprecisely defined that, by some calculations, less than
half of the pitifully small funds that have been allocated for art
are actually going to professional artists and artistic institutions. The reason for this is not hard to determine; it is that
the arts are now being used for political purposes. Perhaps in
order to obscure the fact that the distribution of income in
America varies scandalously, or that the communications
media belong not to the people but rather to certain powerful
corporations, our elected representatives have recently been
trying to democratize the culture—with the result that quality
in art is now less rewarded than its social utility.

This, I believe, accounts also for the current misuse of two
other words—namely "elitist" and "snob"—which are indis-
criminately applied to anyone these days who tries to make an
argument for artistic standards. It is forgotten perhaps that the
word *elite* was once a term not of abuse but rather of commen-
dation; it simply meant leadership. But if the word once implied quality and leadership in quality, it now seems to imply
social standing and self-imposed rule, which further suggests

that we are being confounded in our discussion of the arts by essentially political considerations. Lurking somewhere behind all this invective is the memory, for example, that Hitler once had an "Elite Corps"—and that these were not artists committed to enhancing life, but rather, vicious gangsters dedicated to ending it.

If the word "elitism" has been borrowed from culture and applied to politics, the word "populism" has been borrowed from politics and applied to the arts, with meanings that so far are honorific. It suggests that which is popular—the voice of the people—and the voice of the people, as the saying goes, is the voice of God. That the voice of God twice elected Richard Nixon President of the United States, the second time by the largest plurality in American history, is not always convenient to remember. The cultural populists must provide the illusion that all people are being satisfied, not only in their choice of political leaders, but in their choice of entertainment as well—and this means both a broad range of choice in theatre, movies, TV, music, and painting, and the widest opportunity for personal creative expression, from the neighborhood rock group to the New York Philharmonic.

The impulse behind this is admirable. Still, there is very little danger today that mass taste will go unsatisfied, if only because satisfying this taste is a source of enormous profit for a large number of commercial entrepreneurs. No, the greater danger to a pluralistic society is that the less popular, more unpalatable forms of creative expression will somehow wither and die, partly because genuine works of art are not always accessible to large audiences, being thought difficult, provocative, arcane, or experimental—at least, at first. In the best of all possible worlds, the highest forms of art would be the most popular forms of art, but our world, alas, is not perfect. That is why one turned with such hope to government subsidy—in the expectation that tax dollars would help preserve high art as it now preserves architectural landmarks. If these hopes have begun to die, it is partly because of false, unnatural equations on the level where the money is dispensed—the federal and state level—which are expressed in this flap about elitism.

But, I would ask, who is really more snobbish and patronizing—the one who would bring culture down to the people, or the one who would try to raise people up the culture? Which is the more condescending attitude—the assumption that Shakespeare cannot be understood by the masses unless he is bowdlerized, synopsized, and strained into baby food, or the assumption that great works of art are not fully coherent unless they keep their original form? Chekhov wrote: "We must bring the people up to Gogol, not bring Gogol down to the people." And this is pretty much what Ibsen had in mind when he wrote of "the absolute necessity of democracy . . . to make itself aristocratic."

The words "nobility" and "aristocracy" are freighted with almost as many adverse meanings in our time as "elitist" and "snob"—for we live in an era when what the poet Yeats called "the mad intellect of democracy" has made a mindless egalitarianism the dominant social philosophy. But Ibsen was not saying that superior beings possessed the right to set themselves above the law. He was simply affirming the capacity —indeed, the necessity—of the human race to transform itself into something higher, purer, larger. Shaw said, "I would have my mob all Caesars instead of Toms, Dicks and Harrys." In a speech to the workingmen of Trondhjem, Ibsen himself called for a "new nobility," emphasizing that he meant not a "nobility of birth, nor that of wealth, nor of knowledge, nor of ability or talent. I am thinking of a nobility of character, of a nobility of will and spirit." The aristocracy he called for, then, was a natural nobility that transcended class and inheritance—to be reached through a compound of culture, education, art.

For whatever the blessings and benefits of political democracy, Ibsen saw that the democratization of culture could only be a curse; it signifies the corruption of artistic and intellectual values under pressure from electoral politics. The source of this pressure is a group of politicians installed in office by geographical, ethnic, racial, and sexual constituencies who are now demanding more distribution of federal and state money for the arts and humanities according to geographical, ethnic, racial, and sexual criteria. And so powerful are these pressures on the Hill that the two men newly appointed to take charge of the twin Endowments both seem to feel themselves more accountable to the legislator and the citizen than to the artist or the humanist. In a interview in *U. S. News & World Report,* this is the way Joseph Duffey, the new chairman of the National Endowment for the Humanities, described and confirmed the anti-elitist position. "Those who have accused the Endowment of elitism are saying that humanist scholars need to realize they must listen more to the public. The people of this country are participants in the shaping of our culture and shouldn't be treated as passive recpients of wisdom dispensed by experts. . . . Some of the talk about quality smacks of the worst kind of academic snobbism." *Humanists must listen more to the public. The people are participants in the shaping of the culture.* We've all heard this language before; it is the language of political oratory. But it is the first time, I believe, that it has been applied to artists and humanists, as if they were candidates for office. I fear it will not be the last.

All right, the question remains as to why federal and state tax money should go to artists, scholars, and intellectuals when their works do not directly benefit each and every tax-payer. It is the kind of question, as Ibsen foresaw, that could only be asked in a society blinded by materialism and utilitari-anism, where the state sees art and scholarship as the decora-tions, not the pillars and beams of the edifice. Still, it is a fair question, and needs to be answered. I would say in partial reply that federal and state money should go to these things for the same reason that it now goes to libraries, even though the level of literacy is shamefully low, or to museums, even though most people prefer cartoons to Rembrandt. Some-where, in the back of our minds, we still recognize that minor-ity art and advanced thought are not justified by popularity contests, and that their influence, though not immediately apparent, will ultimately be felt by the masses of people. Christ began with twelve disciples before his teachings became the basis for a world religion; would he have been denied a grant by the National Endowment for the Humanities because the people were not participants in shaping his thought? Joyce, Eliot, Beckett, Van Gogh, Pollock, Stravinsky, indeed all the major modern artists, were barely read or bought or heard for years until they reached a wider audience; should they have been excluded from support because they didn't listen more to the public?

As Ibsen told us, the central obligation of a democracy is to make itself aristocratic; it is to rise above itself, not to lay back on the level of its lowest aspiration and achievement. And it is the central obligation of those responsible for government support of the arts to identify the best that is being thought and created and to nurture the best accordingly. Is that possible in a society dominated by majoritarian consensus rule, where the arts agencies are accountable to the legislators and the legislators are accountable to the voters? Perhaps not, but if not, we must begin thinking about ways to liberate these endowments and commissions from political influence and control. We must begin recognizing that the value of art is not determined by the size of the audience or the contributions to the community. We must begin acknowledging that an artist's vision is often fulfilled only by maintaining a certain aloofness from the state, even from party politics. "I receive more and more proof," wrote Ibsen, "that there is something demoralizing in engaging in politics and joining parties. It will never, in any case, be possible for me to join a party that has the majority on its side. Bjornson says, 'The majority is always right.' And as a practical politician he is bound, I suppose, to say so. I, on the contrary, must of necessity say, 'The minority is always right.' Naturally, I am not thinking of that minority of stand-patters who are left behind by the great middle party that we call liberal; I mean the minority which leads the van and pushes on to points the majority has not yet reached. I mean: that man is right who has allied himself most closely with the future."

Not the conservative then, not the liberal, not even the radical, but rather the visionary artist with a stake in the future, who by fulfilling his vision would fulfill only the social obligation we have a right to ask of him. Can we live with this idea? A tall order in a democracy, but still not an impossible one; and the only hope we have that our country will ultimately fulfill its debt to the artist and understand his purpose.

(1978)

PART III

CULTURAL MOMENTS:
Art and Society

CONTENTS

ONE

Broadway Anglophila

AMERICANS ARE welcoming the British invasion of our theatrical shores with a fervor almost as passionate as that with which, two hundred years earlier, we greeted our freedom from British rule. The triumph on the New York stage in recent years of English plays and players has been followed by audience satisfaction, critical celebration, and industry awards. Broadway—rescued from near-extinction by a succession of London-imported hits—has expressed its gratitude with a number of English Tonys; the Critics' Circle has voted additional prizes; the National Endowment for the Humanities has made a generous grant to the England-based Royal Shakespeare Company in support of its educational tour of our hinterlands; and in a reverse development, Clive Barnes has been honored by the Queen "for his services to British cultural interests in New York." Clearly, everyone is unspeakably happy that such blessings have flowed toward the Broadway stage, and there is no question that the hospitality provided for these productions reflects the characteristic American generosity (one hesitates to add, insecurity) toward cultures more sophisticated than our own. Still, a doubt has been festering in my mind over whether our current theatrical Anglophilia might not be a mixed blessing, a cause for some apprehension along with the rejoicing. I'm not exactly convinced that it testifies to the health either of the New York stage or of its audience.

My feelings on this subject are complicated by the fact that I once served as guest theatre critic on a London newspaper where I had the opportunity to observe, over an extended period, the achievements of English playwrights, actors, directors, and designers. Those familiar with my columns from England may have noticed a growing disenchantment, my enthusiasm for the vigor and variety of production being tempered by a sense that English theatre might be coasting along too much on technical adroitness, sacrificing emotional depth for the sake of style. I never lost my admiration for the structure of the English repertory system; indeed, I continue to believe that some such similar pattern is one prescription for the ailing American theatre. But I thought I discerned, in comparing the 1972–73 London season with previous years, a certain falling off in risk and inspiration from the period when Peter Hall and Peter Brook were bringing such originality and audacity to the Royal Shakespeare Company, when Sir Laurence Olivier was presiding over the early achievements at the National, when George Devine was turning up one brilliant writer after another at the Royal Court. In fact, I ended my sojourn believing that the great days of the English theatre had already passed, and that—with the exception of Edward Bond —few of the interesting English playwrights were advancing beyond their early work.

Returning to the United States, I found Robert Morley issuing jovial TV invitations to London via BOAC; the accomplishments of the British stage had by now become prime tourist attractions for visiting Americans. Inevitably, theatre entrepreneurs began to realize that they could save their audiences plane fare by bringing even more than the customary quota of

English attractions over to New York, and soon, many of the productions of my London year were sitting comfortably on Broadway stages (along with the usual West End commodities like *Absurd Person Singular*): *Sherlock Holmes* and *London Assurance* from the RSC; *Jumpers, The Misanthrope,* and *Equus* from the National; *Scapino* from the Young Vic. Even American companies were taking the opportunity to transfer English plays to New York, with the Long Wharf Theatre bringing its production of *The Changing Room* to the Morosco and *The National Health* to Circle in the Square, while other cities in the country had the opportunity to see another RSC company on tour, with such fine actors as Ian Richardson imparting the secrets of verse-speaking to American drama students.

Obviously, the plays transferred to Broadway, like those the English companies transfer to the West End of London, are going to be the ones with the widest popular appeal, so American audiences have not yet had a chance to see a genuine cross-section of English theatre. But the financial success of these productions will unquestionably attract more plays to these shores in future, which makes it a good possibility that "fringe" groups and experimental playwrights will be represented too. It is paradoxical that English theatre should be helping to stabilize the Broadway economy at the very moment that Britain's economic slump is threatening the financial stability of many of its own companies, but there is no question that—in box-office terms—this theatrical interchange is proving mutually beneficial to both countries.

If for this reason only, it will undoubtedly continue; and I hope what I am about to say will not be construed, in any way, to mean I think it should not continue. But I am compelled to state my conviction that, whatever the advantages to the various parties concerned, these English productions are not advancing American culture an inch. They are, rather, merely filling a vacuum in the commercial theatre that is normally occupied by other forms of casual entertainment.

For the fact is that many of these shows from London are

only lightweight amusements, either in the way they have been written or conceived, and even the more ambitious English plays are often so remote from the American experience that they fail in a vital theatrical function, which is to challenge the audience. Patrons of Broadway have a right to their theatrical pastimes, but for the sake of the record, critics should beware of confusing a pleasant evening in the company of accomplished actors with the kind of probing encounters the theatre provides at its best. To watch Sherlock Holmes locked in combat with the sinister Professor Moriarty, even when played by such an elegant actor as John Wood, is no more to be engaged in a consequential experience than to witness the simpering of Dion Boucicault's fop in *London Assurance,* even in the stylish hands of Donald Sinden. Similarly, it ought to be noted that Molière's *The Misanthrope,* in its present National Theatre adaptation, has almost entirely lost its darkness, ambiguity, and satirical power, becoming instead a crackling wit combat in the English comedy of manners tradition, and that Tom Stoppard's *Jumpers* is philosophy without tears, which reduces weighty intellectual questions to a species of verbal acrobatics.

As for the English plays with deeper purposes, most of them strike me as either too concealed in their intentions or too parochial in their design to leave much mark on Americans; I suspect that such works derive their success less from a capacity to touch New York audiences than from their curiosity as peep shows. How else does one explain the response to Peter Shaffer's *Equus,* where middle-class patrons rise to their feet nightly to cheer over a love affair between a stable boy and a horse—a relationship which the boy's psychiatrist identifies as superior to his own marriage and, by implication, the marriages of the very spectators applauding the play? By contrast with this subtle propaganda for what used to be called deviant sexual behavior, the strategies of David Storey's *The Changing Room* and Peter Nichols' *The National Health* are considerably straightforward. But the first struck me as a work of almost staggering narrowness in its relentless concentration on the

comings and goings of rural rugby players—despite the expertise with which the Long Wharf actors managed to render
nuances of English provincial speech—while the second, as its
title implies, was concerned with the English medical service
as a metaphor for the spiritual health of the country as a whole.

The national health of England, though naturally of interest
to us, is a subject considerably less immediate to our lives than
the national health of America; although our fraternal feelings
for our English-speaking neighbor will always compel concern
for its condition, it may be that such preoccupations are currently substituting for any serious examination of our own
cultural and spiritual state. I write this on the assumption that
a nation's theatre at any given moment is a fairly accurate
barometer of its soul. And just as a surplus of entertainment
on the New York stage may signify a desire for escapism, or
a surplus of revivals a similar impulse toward nostalgia, so a
surplus of English plays and productions may suggest an un-
willingness to confront our own problems and afflictions.

Certainly, there is little evidence on Broadway these days of
any interest in relevant American myths of the kind that gave
Miller's *Death of a Salesman* such power and poignance, that
informed the shattering conflicts of Williams' *A Streetcar Named
Desire,* that provoked the brutal imagery of Van Itallie's *America
Hurrah!,* that permeated the historical fabric of Lowell's *The
Old Glory,* and transcendentally, that elevated O'Neill's personal family nightmare, *A Long Day's Journey Into Night,* into a
universal parable of American life. To those who argue that
such plays are no longer being written, I would answer that
more American playwrights than ever, many of them unrecog-
nized and unsung, are trying to fashion theatrical metaphors
that might accurately catch our historical moment—often
crude, frequently arcane, sometimes painful, but at least aimed
toward making poetry out of the distresses and agonies of our
bewildered nation.

Most of these plays are lying unread on the desks of New
York agents and producers, after limited runs in resident

theatres, or piling up on the beleaguered doorstep of Joseph Papp—one of the few New York producers still inclined to risk his future on them. For it is a fact only vaguely suggested by the statistics (Broadway produced only sixteen new plays of any kind in 1973–74 as compared with seventy produced in the same year by the resident theatres) that the commerical theatre can no longer turn a profit on untried American works, especially those which throw any difficulties at all in the way of its audience.

It is for this reason that Broadway continues its infatuation with the already tested hits of the London stage, while many of the actors who might be qualified to perform in American plays, or to bring an American viewpoint to the classics, are being indoctrinated with British acting techniques, trilling their *r*'s and broadening their *a*'s, bowing and fanning themselves like English lords and ladies. Forgive the note of chauvinism. I don't mean to imply that the English should stop inhabiting our theatres or training our actors, or that Clive Barnes should return his OBE to the Queen. I'm just trying to say that the invasion of the New York stage by the squadrons of England is not simply a source of theatrical pleasure but a cause for cultural concern.

(1973)

TWO

Remakes:
The Retread Culture

We had fed the heart on fantasies,
The heart's grown brutal on the fare.

— W. B. YEATS

IF IT WERE possible to isolate a single identifying characteristic
of American culture over the past decade, it would likely be the
element of reproduction: The representative form of our time
is a *remake*.

By a remake, I mean a cultural work based, however loosely,
upon a previous construct of fiction or legend which refash-
ions the characters, plot, situation, or structure of the original,
usually in the hope of arousing recognition. To take some
obvious examples from the world of entertainment, the television series called *The Hot l Baltimore* was a remake of the play
with the same name by Lanford Wilson. The television series
M*A*S*H does a similar thing with Robert Altman's film. TV's
Happy Days is a thinly disguised remake of the George Lucas
movie *American Graffiti,* in the way it exploits the music and
mores of adolescents in the nineteen-fifties. Mel Brooks's
Young Frankenstein is a comic sequel to the many Frankenstein
monster movies based on Mary Shelley's book (Woody Allen's
Love and Death is a comic satire of virtually the whole of Russian

literature). And the film of *Jaws,* not to mention the Peter Benchley novel from which it is drawn, is a disguised remake both of Ibsen's *An Enemy of the People*—the attempt by officials of a resort town to cover up a threat to its prosperity—and, more obviously, of Melville's *Moby Dick*—the pursuit of a malevolent white marine creature by a fanatical mariner who is eventually destroyed by it.

Much of contemporary American entertainment, in short, is not so much being created as re-created. It is a recycled commodity which moves in dizzying spirals through various media, generally losing depth and detail along the way. Since the remake culture is dependent less on original materials than on existing works, it is a form of parasite, living off a parent body of past achievement. And, as such, the culture is partially reflecting America's current conservative mood. A nation which always looked forward is now in the process of looking backward, with considerable longing for the real or imagined comforts of the past. Where audiences once were eager for what was novel and innovative, they now seem more comfortable with the familiar, as if they wished to escape from contemporary difficulties into the more reassuring territory of the habitual and the known.

This escapist side of the remake culture is certainly reinforced by the current nostalgia boom. Revivals of old stage hits like *No, No, Nanette* and *Irene;* retrospectives of films from the thirties and forties by *auteur-*directors, authentic-looking reconstructions of period styles in new films like *The Sting* and *Godfather II;* revived musical forms like ragtime and fifties rock —all play off a deep American discontent with the present time. So do the "genre" films of industry favorites like Peter Bogdanovich—*What's Up, Doc?, Paper Moon, At Long Last Love* —which seem to be based less on the director's experience of life than on his experience of other movies, as if he had spent his first thirty years imprisoned in a screening room.

The power of this nostalgia has grown so strong that it is now almost impossible to measure. Why, it is even becoming difficult to identify a distinctive look for our age which is not a compound of past fashions. The cut of our trousers, the shape of our dresses, the style of our furs, coiffures, cosmetics and jewelry, our very advertising techniques and printing models, are all derived from earlier periods—a mishmash of the frontier West, Art Deco, and the flapper era (*The Great Gatsby* may have been a failure as a remake film but the "Gatsby look" has made a fortune for the fashion industry).

Obviously, there are commercial reasons behind all of this, and I don't mean to suggest that remakes, revivals, sequels, or reproductions represent anything new. Entrepreneurs have always recognized that what was once successful is likely to be successful again, provided the time is ripe and the consumer is ready. Remakes, in fact, have been the foundation of American musical comedy since its postwar flowering with *Oklahoma!* (a remake of the Lynn Riggs play, *Green Grow the Lilacs*), where for every Broadway musical that used an original book, ten others were drawn from successful novels, short stories and plays. *Cabaret,* for example, began as an Isherwood book, then became a play, a movie of the play, a Broadway musical and, finally, a movie of the musical.

What is different about the remake phenomenon today is its multiplicity and universality. D'Artagnan, after his initial appearance in Dumas, has repeated his adventures in stage plays, Douglas Fairbanks silents and Technicolor talkies, and will no doubt continue riding with his swashbuckling companions as long as entertainment lasts. But the recent Richard Lester version of *The Three Musketeers* consists of two movies, not one, while *The Godfather* appears in *three* parts, including a nine-hour television version of the first two movies with ninety minutes of deleted material restored. Apparently, America's appetite for entertainment is becoming simply insatiable, and as a result, is far outstripping the industry's capacity to generate new products. With all that television time to be filled, all those movie theatres to be occupied, all those records to be sold, remakes not only have become essential to popular media like TV, films, musicals, recordings, fashions and advertising, but are also becoming an important element of scholarship, serious literature, drama, and painting.

What most of these media share is a similar cast of characters—characters who, in turn, were originally brought to prominence by the media. For, if America's hunger for entertainment is strong, its obsession with entertainment figures may be even stronger. I don't think it is unfair to say that the customary favorites of popular culture (Western desperadoes, gangsters, private eyes, policemen, and the like) are gradually being displaced, in the fantasy lives of Americans, by the actors who have represented such characters in the movies or on the home screen. This represents a subtle but significant shift from a previous cultural pattern, for while Americans have always tended to confuse a historical fact with its fictional embodiment—can anyone think about the West any more without calling up images of Gary Cooper walking warily down a dirt street?—they have only recently become preoccupied with the actor's personality to the total exclusion of his or her roles.

Still, it is only natural for remakes to draw attention to the histrionic wrappings rather than the dramatic content: Like other synthetic products, remakes are circulated and sold primarily through their packaging. Constant reproduction of a cultural article has a tendency not just to obscure its original qualities but eventually to obliterate them altogether, so that the consumer's interest is excited only by the surface of the form, and this means the style and gestures of the performers. It is for this reason, I think, that the *dramatis personae* of the remake culture is composed so predominantly of Hollywood movie stars and show-business entertainers. Indeed, nothing better demonstrates the parasitical nature of this culture than the way it is living off its own personalities.

Hollywood, in particular, has grown increasingly absorbed with its own people—just look at the genus of the biographical film. In the thirties and forties, these movies used to center on such straightforward types as statesmen (Raymond Massey's Lincoln), scientists (Paul Muni's Louis Pasteur), composers (Cary Grant's Cole Porter), and inventors (Spencer Tracy's Edison). Now such movies are more likely to be based on the lives of the actors—some of whom may have played those very roles. And while a few Americans may have once thought that Don Ameche invented the telephone system because he played the part of Alexander Graham Bell, they now seem more interested in the movie system that invented *him.*

Films of this kind include one on the relationship between Clark Gable and Carole Lombard, another on the life of W. C. Fields, still others on the careers of Fatty Arbuckle and Rudolph Valentino. Humphrey Bogart invades Woody Allen's fantasies in *Play It Again, Sam,* dressed in the worn raincoat and snap-brim hat he wore in *Casablanca.* Lenny Bruce repeats his routines posthumously, first in a one-man show off-Broadway, then in a Broadway spectacular directed by Tom O'Horgan, and then in a Bob Fosse movie starring Dustin Hoffman. Fanny Brice is resurrected for a Streisand musical on Broadway called *Funny Girl,* which is then turned into a Streisand movie, which in turn generates a Streisand sequel, *Funny Lady.*

Judy Garland is memorialized in dozens of treacly biographies. And Marilyn Monroe becomes the subject of a fictionalized movie biography (Paddy Chayefsky's *The Goddess*) while she is still alive, of a play and TV special (Arthur Miller's *After the Fall*) following her death, and a decade later, of a rock-opera-turned-movie (Ken Russell's production of the Who's *Tommy*). In *Tommy,* she is elevated into an object of religious veneration, carried aloft as an enormous plaster replica of her famous publicity photo in *The Seven-Year Itch* and worshiped by fanatical celebrants as though she were the Madonna. (Like the Virgin Mary, "St. Marilyn" is believed capable of performing miraculous cures.) This recycling of show-business personalities will most likely continue indefinitely: One awaits future films on the lives of Dustin Hoffman and Barbra Streisand, and even future films on the lives of the actors who played *their* parts. But it reveals an interesting feature of our present-day culture, which is the way it exalts entertainment into a religion, with its own icons, relics, rituals, and saints. Admittedly, Americans have always been inclined to worship movie stars —it is a common ailment of those who lead substitute lives— just as fans (a word derived from *fanatic*) have traditionally approached their movie idols with an enthusiasm bordering on the religious, screaming with ecstasy, crushing each other in a desire for closer contact. But this tendency has now reached a point where movie stars are being endowed with magical powers, and provided that they died young enough or under sufficiently tragic circumstances—like James Dean—are even sanctified into figures of mystical veneration.

One finds these attitudes not only among the masses, but also among some influential cultural figures, many of whom express their worship of dead or aging stars by contributing a Hollywood iconography of their own invention. Andy War-hol, in particular, has become identified with the canonization of celebrities—first in his silk-screen tributes to Elizabeth Tay-lor, Marilyn Monroe, and Elvis Presley; then in the half-awe-struck, half-parodic image of the Superstar in his Factory mov-ies; and then in his magazine *Interview,* which features lengthy conversations with fading movie queens. The beatification of vintage Hollywood is a crucial element of Camp (so is the beatification of Tin Pan Alley, a phenomenon associated with performers like Bette Midler and her claque); and it may be that Camp represents an extension of remake nostalgia into the secret corridors of homosexual life. But universities, too, have lately been displaying similar enthusiasms, and not only in their film societies but in their classrooms, where the sleazi-est elements of the culture are becoming the basis for serious academic study. Even a respected writer like Norman Mailer lends his reputation to the practice, turning out a biography of Marilyn Monroe which, though partly written for quick profit, clearly reveals this author's infatuation with the myth and magic of the movie star.

In short, the worship of old entertainment idols has begun to excite not only the popular mind, but also the serious imagination: Imagine William Faulkner writing a biography of Betty Grable, or Picasso doing portraits of Frank Sinatra and Rita Hayworth. (For that matter, try to imagine Saul Bellow writing about Ann-Margret, or Mark Rothko turning out silk-screens of James Dean.) I don't mean to imply that artists in the past have been indifferent to entertainment, or failed to acknowledge the strengths of popular culture. T. S. Eliot and Toulouse-Lautrec were certainly fascinated by the music hall, and paid it tribute in their work. But what they admired in such performers as Marie Lloyd and La Goulue—indeed, what Ernest Hemingway celebrated in his friend Marlene Dietrich—were qualities of suppleness and tough grace, and not their appeal as sex symbols, mass idols, or cult figures.

It is the cultist aspect of the remake culture, however, that seems to attract the modern intelligentsia. Eager to demonstrate their freedom from sober academicism, as well as their relaxation with the products of the mass media, a number of artists and intellectuals have begun to celebrate the passing fads of popular culture—and in a second convolution of elitism no less exclusive than the first, are trying to establish themselves as a new cultural aristocracy by extending the boundaries of artistic endeavor to include whatever happens to be the latest rage. (In a recent article in the *New Republic*, Richard Poirier, professor of English at Rutgers, attacked those "high-culture illiterates" who failed to see that "structurally" there was no difference between the "juxtapositions of style" found in "The Waste Land" and in Bette Midler's latest revue.) Partly as a result, the remake culture now consists not just of commercial adaptations from one medium into another, but also of the manipulation of familiar materials from the mass culture in forms previously associated with high art.

There is no reason why such materials cannot be an imaginative resource for art when laundered of their star-struck impurities. While the underside of the remake phenomenon looks pretty squalid, remakes of one kind or another have always been a commonplace of Western art, particularly before the modern age shattered and dispersed our common dreams. They provided for Europeans what Americans have always longed for: access to a storehouse of knowledge and experience shared by artist and audience alike. The Greeks remade Homeric myths; the Romans remade the Greeks; Molière remade the Romans; the Restoration dramatists remade Molière. Shakespeare remade history, anecdotes, and other plays (*Hamlet* was partly a remake of another *Hamlet,* probably by Thomas Kyd), while his successors remade Shakespeare into domestic tragedies and operas. And the whole contemporary myth movement—in the hands of such composers as Stravinsky, such painters as Picasso, such novelists as Joyce, such dancers as Martha Graham, and such dramatists as Cocteau, Sartre, Anouilh, and Eliot—was an effort to refashion classical myths into statements about modern life, largely through the device of ironic or anachronistic contrasts.

Around the same time, other European artists were growing less interested in the practice of remaking classical myths and historical anecdotes than in remodeling the great works of Western art itself. Painters traditionally had done great work "after" that of a great master. Now playwrights, novelists, stage directors, composers, choreographers, and poets were embarking on works of imaginative reconstruction as well. The pastiche, the echo, the fantasia, the variation on a theme, the adaptation, the directorial essay—all were forms designed both to pay homage to tradition and to subject that tradition to modern interpretation. Bertolt Brecht's plays after *The Threepenny Opera* (a remake of John Gay's eighteenth-century comedy *The Beggar's Opera*) were largely modern adaptations of famous dramatic works, including those of Farquhar, Synge, Gorki and, especially, Shakespeare. Peter Brook's production of *King Lear* was also a kind of free translation of Shakespeare, which made the play look more like a work of Samuel Beckett's. Eugene Ionesco's *Macbett* was a comic drama on the nature of power fashioned as a memorial reconstruction of an early reading of *Macbeth*—or perhaps of Barbara Garson's *MacBird*, another remake of *Macbeth* for contemporary political purposes.

As Mrs. Garson's savage, irresponsible, and oddly prophetic satire suggests, American artists, too, have often felt compelled to remake works from European sources. O'Neill, for example, was continually trying to find a modern equivalent for Greek tragedy (his *Mourning Becomes Electra* is a lumbering version of Aeschylus' *Oresteia,* set in the American Civil War), while Thornton Wilder's *The Skin of Our Teeth* is a remake of Joyce's *Finnegans Wake* and the Bible. Still, American novelists, playwrights, and painters have lately been more inclined to explore the myths and legends of our own historical past. Larry Rivers' painting of "George Washington Crossing the Delaware," not to mention the Kenneth Koch play which it inspired, is a satiric remake of a famous patriotic canvas. And E. L. Doctorow's novel *Ragtime* invents imaginary histories for such turn-of-the-century figures as Houdini, Henry Ford, J. P. Morgan, Sigmund Freud, and Emma Goldman, both for mythic purposes and for the sake of making cogent observations about the development of twentieth-century America.

Moreover, a considerable number of writers for the American stage have begun to use the remake pattern as a basis for a new kind of play. A most prophetic work in this mode was Michael McClure's mid-sixties play, *The Beard,* which showed Jean Harlow in the erotic embrace of Billy the Kid—an early juxtaposition of characters from the worlds of entertainment and from Western legend. Since then, works by Sam Shepard, Arthur Kopit, David Epstein, Thomas Babe, David Freeman, and many others have imaginatively explored similar figures from Hollywood and the West. These plays, most of them unfamiliar to the majority of Americans, are by now so common as to constitute an unacknowledged movement—a movement designed to de-heroicize the legendary American past.

But it is the potential of this movement, rather than the plays themselves (which are of varying quality), that suggests how remakes can achieve some value for our culture beyond their function as assembly-line commodities. By bringing onto the stage a group of characters already known by the audience, the American playwright can proceed with his thematic purpose without wasting time over such realistic conventions as linear plot construction and psychological character development; he can escape from domestic restrictions and penetrate the fabric of American history; he can roam free over space and time for the purpose of exploring the roots of our current afflictions.

Too often, it must be admitted, the familiar associations aroused in the audience are expected to do the playwright's work, so that the play tends to grow limp once the shock of recognition wears off. But the effort itself is significant; it reflects a need to regain for the theatre some of the advantages that Greek mythology lent to the work of Sophocles, or Tudor history to the plays of Shakespeare—common access to a familiar terrain from which the artist can make imaginative leaps.

Still, the terrain is full of potholes, for there is a vast difference between fantasies and myths. Myths reveal reality, fantasies only blur it; Aphrodite tells us something about the fierce power of passion, "St. Marilyn" only about the exacting price of fame. The figures of the American legendary landscape are often such manufactured personalities that they wash out reality altogether, and the preponderance of movie stars in the remake culture suggests that our view of life is cosmetic: We prefer reality when it is mascaraed, manicured, and coiffed.

We prefer, in short, the glossy surface to the scarred interior, and that is why it is hard to be too sanguine about the future of remakes in America. A people who regard their present circumstances with such fear and hatred are not likely to contemplate their past with any degree of truth, nor is the synthetic culture likely to offer much in the way of genuine revelation or insight. For many Americans, the most satisfying embodiment of our history is to be found in Disney World: spanking-clean streets and neat frame houses, horse-drawn wagons and artificial landscapes; robot Presidents making stiff welcoming gestures while cassette recordings sanctimoniously intone portions of their speeches. Disney World is the culmination of our nostalgia, the ultimate remake. It is a homogenized Utopia engineered with technological perfection by the entertainment industry, which removes from history anything that might threaten, deepen, or distemper our dreams.

This architecture of escape is the logical extension of a culture of escape, and it suggests that we have finally come to the point where, conditioned by millions of hours in front of the home screen, at the movies and under the headphones, we have actually come to prefer reproductions to originals. (Perhaps this is why, instead of looking at something beautiful, we point our cameras at it, so as to look at the pictures instead.) And, as reluctant as we are to experience a new artistic work, we are even more resistant to a new idea, a new approach, a new policy. We have become paralyzed as a nation, unable to move in any direction, plagued by problems but will-less to solve them. Instead, we grow fat on fantasies, drugged by placebos, absorbing images, media-soaked.

Remakes, then, will no doubt continue to be the basic pabulum of our popular culture. Do they offer no opportunities at all for the serious artist? I have already suggested some of the ways in which the past can be used as a path to contemporary understanding instead of as a yellow brick road to escape. Perhaps the most significant model, in the theatre, is still Robert Lowell's 1964 masterpiece, *The Old Glory.* A trio of short plays based on Hawthorne and Melville stories, *The Old Glory* is not simply a slavish recasting of familiar works from the American Lit. syllabus, but rather a heavily charged, entirely original examination of the American character at three different points in its historical development. Particularly in *Benito Cereno,* the last play in the trilogy, set in 1800 aboard a ship on which slaves being brought from Africa stage a rebellion, Lowell uses Melville's theme—the shadow cast over the civilized mind by the primitive darkness—in order to pursue his own— the brutal American treatment of the Negro which has sparked our perilous present-day racial confrontations. Thus, by means of his own chilling prose style and metaphorical invention, this gifted poet and playwright has discovered a dynamic function for the remake—not to sink us further into narcosis and complacency, but rather, by superimposing the present onto the past, to unearth the seeds of our current discords.

So, despite the power of the commercial remake juggernaut, alternatives are still possible. On the one hand, a starry-eyed celebration of celebrity, on the other, a cold-eyed investigation of our legendary and historical past; on the one hand, a varnishing of our national wrinkles, on the other, an exposure of the roots of our present problems.

The impulse behind the production of remakes suggests not only a desire to avoid reality but, in some degree, a compulsion to face it, for it reflects a yearning for active heroes that is not being satisfied by contemporary cultural or political figures. Whether this will issue in more commercial retreads or in new forms, whether in Camp superstars or in figures worthy of our admiration, whether in fantasies that brutalize the heart or myths that reveal the soul, is still something of an open question. The odds are long, and the dice are loaded, but there is still an outside chance that remakes will not just continue to accommodate the American desire for escape, but will help us in the much more difficult, much more necessary task of reawakening our sleeping nation, and shaking it back to life.

(1975)

THREE

═══════════════════════════

Theatre in the Age of Einstein: The Crack in the Chimney

IN THE SECOND act of Ibsen's *The Master Builder,* Halvard Solness endeavors to explain to his young admirer, Hilda Wangel, the origin of his peculiarly lucky career as a builder. It had all begun with a fire in his own house, a fire which caused the death of his children and turned his wife into a living corpse, but which also gave him his first chance to exercise his building talents. The curious thing about this scene is the manner in which he describes the cause of that fatal blaze.

SOLNESS: You see, the whole business revolves around little more than a crack in a chimney.

HILDA: Nothing else?

SOLNESS: No; at least not at the start. . . . I'd noticed that tiny opening in the flue long before the fire. Every time I wanted to start repairing it, it was exactly as if a hand was there, holding me back. So nothing came of it.

HILDA: But why did you keep postponing?

SOLNESS: Because I went on thinking, through that little

black opening, I could force my way to success—as a builder.

So far, nothing unusual. The passage looks like a perfectly conventional piece of exposition, with the playwright demonstrating how the past influences the present—how Solness began his career and developed his guilty conscience. A crack in the chimney, leading to a dreadful fire. An opportunity to subdivide the burnt-out area into building lots. A new reputation as a builder of suburban homes.

But then something extraordinary happens in the scene, as Ibsen proceeds to annihilate his own very carefully fashioned causal construction.

HILDA: But wait a minute, Mr. Solness, how can you be so sure the fire started from that little crack in the chimney?
SOLNESS: I can't, not at all. In fact, I'm absolutely certain it had nothing whatever to do with the fire. . . .
HILDA: *What?*
SOLNESS: It's been proved without a shadow of a doubt that the fire broke out in a clothes closet, in quite another part of the house.

Hilda's exclamation of astonishment is shared by a chorus of readers and spectators, for the play seems to have taken a very mischievous turn. But Ibsen is not intending to be perverse here. Quite the contrary, what he is suggesting is entirely consistent with his poetic apprehension of reality and with the metaphysical impulse animating all his plays, including his so-called "social-realistic" drama. The determination of guilt and its expiation may still constitute the moral quest of his characters, but Ibsen obviously believes that the sources of this guilt are not very easily accessible to the inquiring mind.

What Ibsen is anticipating, in this passage, is the significant turn that the theatre was to take sometime around the end of the nineteenth century, in common with similar developments in science, philosophy, and literature—the artistic departure which was responsible, in part, for the movement called modernism, and which influenced the work of a number of major European dramatists, among them Strindberg, Pirandello, Beckett, Ionesco, and Handke.

For Ibsen has quietly proceeded to undermine a basic assumption of the naturalist universe—namely, that cause A precedes consequence B, which in turn is responsible for the catastrophe C. Isn't it possible, he suggests, that A has nothing whatever to do with B, much less with C, regardless of the apparent evidence? Isn't it possible that events are so multiple and complex that the human intelligence may never be able to comprehend the full set of causes preceding any situation, consequence, or feeling? Ibsen, in short, is attempting to repeal the simple, fundamental law of cause-and-effect which has been an unquestioned statute at least since the Enlightenment —the law that ruled the linear, logical, rationalistic world of literature, and, in particular, the Western literature of guilt. In its place, he is reconfirming the unknowable, ineffable secrets underlying the will of Nature.

All of Ibsen's plays contain religious elements, but *The Master Builder* is clearly his most religious play since *Brand.* What the playwright is trying to do through the character of his ruthless, guilty hero, Solness, is to challenge the orthodox pieties at the same time that he is preserving the romantic mysteries. The purpose of the universe, the structure of character, the nature of sin—all are beyond the reach of traditional concepts; they can be determined only through the artist's intuition, and then only darkly. And the task of the modern artist is to help humankind move beyond the sterile cycle of guilt and expiation, which is one of the offshoots of cause-and-effect thinking. Hilda exhorts Solness to challenge God by developing a robust Viking conscience. Ibsen exhorts us to become gods by transcending our sense of guilt, through a gargantuan effort of the will and the inspired intelligence. Whether this is finally possible is open to serious doubt. But one thing is certain: The old rationalistic assumptions will no longer serve the modern understanding. Indeed, they can only compound ignorance and point us toward false paths.

Ibsen's proposals are revolutionary. They challenge not only conventional theatre, but conventional religion, conventional psychology, conventional social theory as well. Nevertheless, these proposals are actually a return to the assumptions of an earlier age of mystery, which held sway before the advent of Newtonian physics, Cartesian logic, and behavioral psychology. The drama of the Greeks and Elizabethans, for example, is rarely causal in our modern sense: Human motives are sometimes so numerous that latter-day commentators find it hard to give the characters credibility. Clytemnestra offers not one but five or six reasons for killing Agamemnon; Iago mentions so many motives for hating Othello that Coleridge was led to speak of the senseless motive-hunting of a "motiveless malignity"; and T. S. Eliot criticized Shakespeare for failing to give Hamlet an "objective correlative," meaning simply that he found Hamlet's feelings to be in excess of his situation.

While contemporary social scientists are busy rooting around in search of causal explanations for poverty, crime, neurosis, and madness, great artists have traditionally understood that the true explanations are beyond concepts of blame. As Shakespeare's Edmund puts it, "This is the excellent foppery of the world, that, when we are sick in fortune—often the surfeit of our own behavior—we make guilty of our disasters the sun, the moon, and the stars. . . . Pfut! I should have been that I am, had the maidenliest star in the firmament twinkled on my bastardizing."

European drama has recaptured this understanding also, at least since the middle of the last century, when Ibsen—along with Nietzsche and Kierkegaard—threw down a gauntlet not only before orthodox religion, but before the prevailing liberal ideology of the nineteenth and twentieth centuries, meanwhile reducing the middle-class living room to a pile of rubble and exposing domestic realism as a cardboard illusion.

A quick look at the history of our own theatre reveals that American drama has been very slow in rising to this challenge, or even in revealing any awareness of it. Just as the dominant strain of our religious life has been a form of Judaeo-Christian Puritanism, and the dominant strain of our politics a form of liberal reform democracy, so the dominant strain of our stage has been social, domestic, psychological, and realistic—which is to say, *causal*—and its dominant theme, the excavation, exposure, and expiation of guilt. The fires that burn through most American plays have been caused by that crack in the chimney, and the guilty conscience of our theatrical characters can usually be traced to a single recognizable event.

This is particularly striking when one considers how many playwrights in the mainstream of American drama have thought themselves to be writing consciously in an Ibsenite tradition. And I speak now not just of the dramatists of the pre–World War II period—such social-minded writers as Clifford Odets, Sidney Howard, Maxwell Anderson, Robert Sherwood, Lillian Hellman, Irwin Shaw, and John Steinbeck—but also of the postwar "mood" playwrights—including such psychological writers as Tennessee Williams, Arthur Miller, William Inge, Paddy Chayefsky, William Gibson, Frank Gilroy, and, more recently, Lanford Wilson, Mark Medoff, Paul Zindel, Michael Cristofer, and David Rabe.

Even the progenitor of our drama, Eugene O'Neill—though he began writing under the strict influence of Nietzsche and Strindberg—became a causal dramatist in his last plays, when he was writing under the influence of Ibsen. In his greatest play, indeed the greatest play ever written by an American, *A Long Day's Journey Into Night*, O'Neill proceeds to weave a close fabric of causality; every character in the play is suffering pangs of remorse and every character is trying to determine the root cause of his guilt. If the blighted house of Tyrone is misbegotten, then every one of the family is implicated in the other's hell. Each separate action radiates outward into myriad branches of effects, and characters interlock, imprisoned in each other's fate.

My point reflects not on the quality of this play, which is a masterpiece, but rather on the fact that *A Long Day's Journey Into Night* is so remorselessly American in its concentration on the sources of guilt, and on the painful confrontations between parents and their children. These emphases are also evident in the work of an even more conscientious disciple of Ibsen—Arthur Miller—who, along with Tennessee Williams, has been the most celebrated postwar American dramatist, and the strongest influence on the American realist theatre. Miller first broke upon the contemporary consciousness, in fact, with a play that draws heavily from such middle Ibsen works as *The Wild Duck, Pillars of Society,* and *An Enemy of the People*—namely, *All My Sons.* Located in a middle-class living room around the end of World War II, this play had the task of identifying the guilt and establishing the responsibility of its elder protagonist, a wealthy manufacturer named Joe Keller. Keller has served a short time in the penitentiary, having been convicted of increasing his profits by manufacturing faulty cylinder heads for aircraft engines; these have caused the deaths of a number of American fighter pilots. Keller's older son, Larry, is missing in action and, at one point, the characters consider the possibility that the same faulty parts may have been responsible for his death as well. By the play's end, we learn that the causal connection exists, but in indirect form: Upon discovering that his father was responsible for the deaths of his comrades, Larry committed suicide by purposely crashing his plane. After a confrontation with his surviving son, Chris, Keller is forced to recognize that he is responsible for more than the lives of his immediate family—that the victims are "all my sons." He expiates his guilt through his own suicide.

It is easy enough to score points on Miller's dramaturgy, which often seems as faulty as Joe Keller's airplane parts. But my quarrel is not with the far-fetched plotting of a young and relatively inexperienced writer; his work is to grow considerably more convincing as his career progresses. No, my point is, rather, that *All My Sons* is based on assumptions and conventions which, regardless of how the playwright matures, remain central to all his work, as well as to most mainstream American drama—assumptions and conventions which are virtually anathema to Ibsen. For Miller is firmly wedded to simple theatrical causality, whether the sequential links are direct or indirect, and his plays never escape the kind of connection he establishes in *All My Sons,* between Joe Keller's crime and Larry Keller's air crash. The action A precedes the consequence B, which leads inevitably to the guilty catastrophe C.

And the catalyst in this chemical mixture is almost invariably the protagonist's son, who manages to bring the plot from a simmer to a boil. In fact, the typical Miller drama has a code which might be deciphered thus: The son exposes the father's guilt and shows him the way to moral action, and sometimes inadvertently to suicide. Take Miller's most famous play— often called the finest tragedy of modern times—*Death of a Salesman.* The familiar main plot concerns the false values of Willy Loman, but the character who confronts Willy with the fraudulence of his life is Biff, Willy's older son. Once extremely close to his father, Biff now has grown estranged from Willy, for reasons that Miller chooses to keep hidden until the end of the play. Something has happened between them, something which has affected not only their relationship, but Biff's entire mature life; he has broken off a promising high school career and drifted aimlessly around the country. This, in turn, has had a powerful influence on Willy's life, since Biff once represented his main hope for the future. Ineluctably, the play brings us toward the revelation buried inside this family mystery: Coming to visit his father in Boston one day, Biff discovers that Willy has a woman in his room.

Clearly, Miller is willing to risk a great deal of credibility in order to establish a moral showdown between father and son. Consider how much of the plot, theme, and character development hinge on this one climactic hotel-room encounter. *Death of a Salesman* purports to be about false American values of success, but beneath the sociological surface lies the real drama—a family drama of guilt and blame. The source of Biff's hero worship, the model for his own life and behavior, has been discovered in Boston being unfaithful to Mom.

In short, the premises underlying Miller's themes and actions are not Ibsenite in the least. They belong to the eighteenth century, which is to say to the age of Newton, rather than to the twentieth, which is the age of Einstein. And Miller's theatrical Newtonianism remains an essential condition of his style, whether he is writing about the Salem witch hunts, or about the guilt and responsibility of those implicated in the Nazi crimes, or about self-destructive glamour queens, or about East European dissidents. In each of Miller's plays—indeed, in most of the plays of his contemporaries and disciples—every dramatic action has an equal and opposite reaction. It is the crack in the chimney that sends the house up in flames.

So prevalent is this pattern in mainstream American drama that even now, toward the end of the 1970s, our most highly acclaimed playwrights are still shaping their works to sequential diagrams. The style of our drama has admittedly undergone something of an exterior change; its causal pattern is occasionally more elliptical than in Miller's work; and the familiar fourth-wall realism is occasionally broken by stylistic devices. But these are changes touching the surface rather than the hearts of these plays. More often than not, American mainstream dramatists continue to explore the causes behind their effects; the event to be excavated is still the guilt of the (generally older generation) protagonists; and the drama retains the air of a courtroom, complete with arraignments, investigations, condemnations, indictments, and punishments.

Take David Rabe, perhaps the most typical and the most highly esteemed of the younger generation playwrights. Rabe has been called the likely successor to Eugene O'Neill—but a perfunctory glance at his accomplishments soon reveals that he has a closer relative in Arthur Miller. Like Miller, Rabe is fundamentally a social dramatist, fashioning vague attacks on the system; like Miller, he identifies the nexus of corruption in the heart of the family; and like Miller, he will occasionally make modest departures from domestic realism in order to indict his middle-class characters for the crimes of the nation at large.

In Rabe's case, these crimes are almost invariably linked with the Vietnam war—an event that continues to obsess him, not surprisingly, since he is a veteran of that war. In *Sticks and Bones,* for example, he sketches a semisurrealist portrait of middle-class guilt, pitting a returning blind soldier (also named David) against the members of his immediate family: Ozzie, his father; Harriet, his mother; and Rickie, his guitar-playing brother. These names, recognizable from a popular sit-com series, promise a satire on TV—but Rabe is more interested in savaging the people who watch it. In the background, visible only to the blind son throughout most of the play, is Zung, a Vietnamese woman with whom David had lived during his service abroad.

Rabe's larger purpose depends on our believing that Ozzie, Harriet, and Rick represent a typical American family, but before long, Ozzie is strangling Zung, outraged by her sexual relationship with David, Harriet is revealing a callous cruelty that belies her pose of maternal self-sacrifice, and Rickie is helping David to cut his wrists in full view of his approving parents. What Rabe is attempting to symbolize is the hatred and savagery that middle-class Americans feel not only toward foreigners but toward members of their immediate families, in order to identify racism as the fundamental cause of the Vietnam war.

Rabe's "poetic" and "surrealist" devices are actually only stratagems, permitting him to generalize about his characters and his themes, while his political concerns seem to have less inner importance for him than his domestic interests. What he has actually created is a relatively straightforward family drama about the confrontation between an indignant radical young man and his unfeeling conservative parents, with a crisis not very different from the climactic scenes in *All My Sons* and *Death of a Salesman.* A son uncovers the source of his father's guilt and thereupon proceeds to lecture him about his past and present errors, and, by extension, the errors of the country he represents.

What is remarkable is the way in which American audiences have sat still for *their* portion of guilt, not only failing to rise to these baited challenges, but conferring fame, fortune, and Pulitzer Prizes on the writers who savage them most. At least one member of this audience—himself a young writer named Christopher Durang—has refused Rabe's indictment. In parodying the Western theatre of guilt, Durang has begun to suggest one of the directions our drama might take, were that crack in the chimney ever to be repaired. Durang's play is entitled *The Vietnamization of New Jersey,* and it is a satire of such ferocity that it runs roughshod not only through the conventions of *Sticks and Bones,* but through some of our most cherished liberal illusions.

Durang is a lineal descendant of Lenny Bruce, which is to say he trespasses on forbidden ground, skirting perilously close to nihilism. Still, Durang's nihilism is earned; like Bruce, he obviously suffers for it. The satire in *The Vietnamization of New Jersey* has been called collegiate, but it is rarely facile, and it is never self-righteous. Durang's comedy, at its best, has deep roots in a controlled anger, which can only be expressed and purged through a comedy of the absurd.

The Vietnamization of New Jersey is set in a suburban American living room, piled to the ceiling with the detritus of our consumer culture: two hair dryers, three TV sets, an outsized roto-grill, sculptured ducks in flight over the fireplace. Seated at the breakfast table are Rabe's benighted family, now renamed Ozzie Ann, Harry, and Et, their teenage delinquent son. Et is pouring cornflakes down his trousers and eating his breakfast out of his crotch. Hazel, the black maid, clears the table by ripping off the cloth, dropping coffee, toast, and cereal into the laps of her employers, whom she proceeds to indict as malignant symbols of white America.

Into this disaster area comes David, home from the war, with his Vietnamese wife, Liat. Both are blind, which David demonstrates by walking into the refrigerator. Et moralizes: "The fact that they're blind literally in a way points to the fact that we and the American people are blind literally. We suffer, I think, a moral and philosophical blindness." Liat has married David because he is "the best damn stick man in the U.S. Army"— as a result, she can't remember if his name is Cholly or Joe. When they both fall into the family septic tank, Et draws the inevitable political conclusion that this symbolizes the way America is mired in the Vietnam war. Eventually, we learn that Liat is actually a girl named Maureen O'Hara from Schenectady, who went to Vietnam because she wanted to break into American musicals like *The King and I.*

David suffers a nervous breakdown when he learns that he can no longer use Liat to excoriate his parents' guilt, and spends the next four years hiding under the breakfast table. The coming of inflation reduces the family's fortunes: For Thanksgiving, they can afford only Campbell's Chunky Soup. Creditors repossess not only the furniture, but the walls of the set as well. Harry loses his job and shoots himself, ruining Ozzie Ann's nice new rug. The family is saved by Harry's brother, Larry, a Mafia hit man, also a sergeant in the Army reserves. Dressed like General Patton in jodphurs and a bright chrome helmet, Larry brings order back into the household, teaching the family discipline, seducing Liat with chocolates and nylons, and catching David in a bear trap. At the end of the play, with everything having returned to normalcy, David decides to burn himself to death, and while Hazel regales the audience with ludicrous Bicentennial Minutes, the family admires the lovely orange glow that David is making in the sky.

Durang owes a certain debt to Ionesco in his manipulation

of the absurd, but his style is peculiarly American. What he is obviously satirizing here is the heavy-handed symbolism, the piety, the self-satisfaction, the ponderous confrontations, and the cut-rate merchandising of guilt and indignation that pervade so much linear American drama, at the same time that he is demolishing the clichés about the Vietnam war expressed both by the right and the left. With *The Vietnamization of New Jersey,* Durang has declared a separate peace, and as far as American culture is concerned, has finally brought the Vietnam war to a close.

Insofar as Durang belongs to a previous Absurd tradition, however, he breaks no new formal ground. One dramatist who is beginning to turn over the theatrical topsoil is Sam Shepard, a writer with an unusually large body of mythic material, considering his comparative youth. In common with a number of young playwrights today, Shepard is exploring ways to find shortcuts through the habitual terrain of plot, character, and theme, primarily through the use of legendary material, borrowed from Western myths and myths of the movies, including gangster films, horror films, and science fiction. By bringing recognizable figures onto the stage from popular culture, Shepard and his followers are able to dispense with illusionary settings and obligatory exposition, fashioning instead a drama which is metaphorical and mysterious, with the ambiguous reverberations of poetry.

In one of his more recent plays, *Suicide in B Flat,* Shepard goes one step further, attempting to achieve the condition of music—particularly the spacey effects of progressive jazz. As a matter of fact, jazz of this kind is played throughout the evening, by a pianist who sits onstage with his back to the audience, accompanying the actors. The play takes the form of an improvisation, within the genre of pulp fiction. Two detectives, with mysterious links to government agencies, are trying to solve a mystery regarding Niles, a celebrated jazz composer, whose corpse has been found in his room. Was his death the result of murder or suicide? The gumshoes cannot decide, and the chalked outline of his body on the floor does not reveal the secret. When these conventional-minded working stiffs are joined by a suicidal female bass player and a skinny spaced-out saxophonist who blows soundless music (Niles's jazz is so advanced that even dogs can't hear it), the whole business begins to get beyond them. One of the detectives starts wrestling with his own hand which, having developed a life of its own, is trying to stab him with a knife. The other grows increasingly paralyzed as the sax player sits on his lap and tortures him with his protruding bones.

Niles appears, invisible to all except a nervous young groupie who accompanies him. He may be dead, or—perhaps the same thing—he may have gone over into another space-time dimension; Shepard never tells us. But before Niles can rest, he must annihilate a series of identities that prevent him from achieving authenticity. By the end of the play, Niles has walked through the walls of his room to accept the guilt for his own death. As the detectives lead him away in handcuffs, the upstage pianist concludes with the haunting strains of his own jazz.

Like much of Shepard's work, the play is a hallucination and therefore not readily available to logical explanation. Still, the themes curl up like vapor from the performance: The problems caused by celebrity in America, the necessity to transcend despair, the need of the artist to break down false self-images in order to create a genuine vision. And it is interesting that, in the act of disintegrating the causal conventions of realistic theatre, Shepard has also managed to reinterpret the conventional drama of guilt. For *Suicide in B Flat* is a self-accusation, rather than an indictment, in which guilt becomes the price we pay for being alive.

With Sam Shepard, the American theatre takes a step beyond the Newtonian universe into a world of dream, myth, and inner space. With Robert Wilson, it leaps into the universe of Einstein, developing new dimensions of outer space and fractured time.

My reference to Einstein's universe is not gratuitous. All of Wilson's bizarre theatre pieces involve a relativity-influenced temporal and spatial sense, and one of his latest works—a dance-opera-drama created in collaboration with the brilliant composer Philip Glass—is actually entitled *Einstein on the Beach*.

This five-hour meditation shows the influence of Einstein both in its physics and its spirit. In fact, every one of the actors has been made up to resemble Albert Einstein (they are dressed in suspenders, gray pants, and tennis shoes), and the principal soloist, like Einstein a violinist, wears a flowing white wig and a bushy white mustache.

The opera brings us from the world of the locomotive, which is to say the machinery of the Industrial Revolution, to the world of the spaceship, Einstein's culminating gift to the twentieth century. Built around three separate settings—a train, a courtroom, and a field—connected by little dialogues in front of the curtain, called "knee plays," the work dramatizes (so subtly one absorbs it through the imagination rather than the mind) the change in perception—especially perception of time—that accompanied this technological development. The interminable length of the performance, therefore, becomes a condition of its theme, as do the strange schematic settings, the vertical and horizontal shafts of lights, and the apparently meaningless snatches of dialogue.

The Train scene at the beginning of the play gives some sense of its style. A little boy stands atop a crane, throwing paper airplanes into the air every five or ten minutes; a woman dances diagonally back and forth the length of the stage, spasmodically waving her arms. Two people create and examine a triangle made of string. A man listens to the sound of a seashell. A huge locomotive cutout, manned by an engineer with a pipe, inches forward, disappears in a blackout, then appears a little further forward, always preceded by billows of smoke. The scene takes over an hour to perform.

Other episodes include the trial of a woman, presumably Patty Hearst, who is condemned and sentenced by a robot jury, and by two bewigged judges (an old black man and a child), a dance sequence in a field culminating with the appearance of a spaceship model on a string sliding across the upper proscenium, and a second train scene, this time with the caboose facing the audience, involving some inexplicable conflict between a man and a woman. The final big scene provides the most striking effect of the evening: The stage is converted into the huge interior of a spaceship, propelled by the entire cast, in which plastic capsules containing human bodies move laterally across the length of the stage, and the statistics of the Hiroshima disaster are projected on a scrim. We have been involved in a progress from locomotive to rocket propulsion, from paper airplanes to space travel, from firecrackers to nuclear explosions. And yet, as the final knee play demonstrates —bringing a bus cutout into view, driven by a man who tonelessly recites the lyrics of a romantic song—our language for love has remained essentially the same.

Some of this seems irritatingly self-indulgent; but most of it is extremely evocative for those who have the patience to receive its images. Wilson is beginning to fashion some very powerful visual metaphors which have been surpassed, I believe, only in the movie that obviously influenced *Einstein on the Beach*—namely, Stanley Kubrick's *2001*. It is true that the visual effects are the most dazzling and original aspects of the work: Wilson is essentially a painter who paints in motion. But with this work, he is launching the theatre into the unknown and the unknowable, in a way that makes our contemporary domestic plays look like ancient artifacts of a forgotten age.

These three playwrights, then, have virtually demolished the "tasteless parlor" of the illusionistic theatre, and not simply through the let's-pretend devices associated with, say, the theatre of Thornton Wilder. Durang, in an excess of satiric rage, literally knocks down the walls of the family home; Shepard walks his characters through those walls, like poltergeists from another space-time continuum; and Wilson is beginning to investigate the outer reaches of the expanding universe. By leaping beyond the physical confines of the kitchen, the bedroom, and the living room, these writers are transcending the thematic limitations imposed by those rooms as well. Artists working in other forms have been responsive to the kinds of discoveries now affecting the modern consciousness—relativity theory, black holes, quasars, bends in time, antimatter, ESP, and the like. Now the theatre is showing some sign that it has not remained impassive before the liberating new possibilities of the imagination.

And that has been the destiny of all great art—theatrical, literary, visual, or musical; ancient or modern—to expand rather than to limit the structure of imagination. The strict laws governing so much modern drama provide an atmosphere of safety and predictability, but only at the cost of severe restrictions on the possibilities of creation. To live in uncertainty in such insecure, inchoate times as ours is to live in fear and trembling. But what the poet Keats called the "negative capability"—meaning our capacity to function with doubts and ambiguities—remains an essential condition of the poetic imagination. Like Molière's Monsieur Jourdain, we are beginning to discover that we have been speaking prose all our lives —and we have been listening to too much prose as well. But the nonlinear theatre fulfills some of the conditions of poetry by introducing us to the unexpected, and bringing us beyond the prosaic formulas of our social-psychological universe.

For it is constructed on a metaphor, the channel through which artists find their way to a hidden reality inaccessible to barren explanations and causal links. I hope it is obvious that I am not arguing here for obfuscation or obscurantism. If excessive rationalizing is the bane of modern theatre, then there is an equal problem in formulating mystery for its own sake, as I believe Edward Albee and Harold Pinter are sometimes prone to do. The true dramatic poet understands that metaphor is a tool with which to reveal rather than to obscure, a key to turn those locks that remain impervious to conceptual thought.

And, finally, this metaphorical theatre will help to free us from the facile guilt-mongering of our accusatory playwrights. Rhetoric—as W. B. Yeats told us in a famous passage—proceeds from the quarrel with others, poetry from the quarrel with ourselves. The rhetorical indignation so familiar to twentieth-century drama is a result of a failure to understand that the accusing finger may not belong to a blameless hand. Master Builder Solness denounced himself for failing to repair that crack in the chimney, even though he knew full well it had nothing to do with the fire that destroyed his house. Thus, he accepted his own guilt—a condition of being human—and thus, he transcended it—a condition of being an artist. Only through this double responsibility could he preserve the mysteries without losing his humanity, and go on to create a penetrating new art.

(1978)

FOUR

The Fate of Ibsenism

WHENEVER GROUPS of people join together to pay homage to the achievements of some literary artist, I cannot help thinking of what T. S. Eliot wrote about the reputation of Ben Jonson: "To be universally accepted; to be damned by the praise that quenches all desire to read the book; to be afflicted by the imputation of virtues which excite the least pleasure; and to be read only by historians and antiquaries—this is the most personal conspiracy of approval."

The celebration of the 150th anniversary of Ibsen's birth has made us conscious that his reputation is considerably more muscular than that. After all, he is being read by other than antiquaries and historians—by those of us who teach him, for example, and by the students of those of us who teach. But I cannot throw off the suspicion that, like Ben Jonson, Henrik Ibsen may have become something of an academic icon, who has entered our libraries without finding a place in our minds, a familiar figure in our classroom, but a relative stranger to our stage. It is true that the Ibsen Sesquicentennial is at present inspiring productions here and there in various parts of the country, as did the Pirandello Centennial some years ago. But if the productions of *Henry IV* and *Right You Are* in 1967 are any guide, the performances today of *Peer Gynt* and *The Wild Duck* and *A Doll's House* will not be followed by much in the way of further celebration, once the candles on the cake have been extinguished and the birthday party is over. For Ibsen is now beginning to suffer the deadly fate of the classic author—to be included in the anthologies and excluded from the imaginative life of the people, to be universally accepted without being much liked or understood.

I can think of two reasons for this unfortunate condition, one being formal, the other philosophical. Certainly, the stylistic breakthroughs of the modern Ibsen have been achieved at a high price, for his decision to subordinate his expansive poetic imagination, fully expressed in such dramatic poems as *Brand* and *Peer Gynt,* to prose stories about contemporary life, in such plays as *Ghosts* and *Hedda Gabler,* resulted in a severe restriction of creative freedom, at least on the surface of his work. The landscape of theatrical realism, once so novel and vital, now tends to seem stale and unconvincing, particularly since the invention of motion-picture photography. And Ibsen's decision to set his scene in the contemporary drawing room, piled high with bourgeois upholstery, where the action is continually being punctuated by interludes over herring salad and Tokay wine, made it likely that the attention of the audience would be distracted by contemporary details, that the eye would make listless the mind and the imagination. Ibsen embraces these scenic limitations for the sake of establishing a deceptive surface, which he hoped to penetrate through revelation and exposure—as if to say, the reality you perceive is an illusion or chimera, with as much fidelity to the truth as matter has to Plato's Idea. Ibsen believed that the poet's task is "not to reflect but to *see.*" By this he meant, to see through the appearances of the surface to the deeper truths beneath.

For such a strategy, as I said, he paid a price. By developing the style called realism, by inhabiting his role as "father of the modern drama," Ibsen became imprisoned, against his will, in what Henry James would later term the "tasteless parlor." And generation after generation of admirers and enemies alike, of both readers and audiences, would begin to consider Ibsen as the playwright of everyday life—"the chosen author," as W. B. Yeats called him, "of very clever young journalists," describing reality, to recall Synge's scornful phrases, "in joyless and pallid words." And what of his characters? Fat, belching burghers in three-piece suits, emancipated women slamming doors on unfeeling husbands, an adolescent girl blinking away her growing blindness, a drunken doctoral student leaving his manuscript to be thrown into the fire, an aging architect falling off a tower to impress his young admirer, a bankrupt industrialist pacing back and forth upstairs while the women below discuss his life. A menagerie of domestic animals, desperately trying to get some edge on their teeth, some point on their claws, some sheen to their fur, but ultimately too tame to do more than evacuate their energy in long expository barks and growls.

It goes without saying that such a perception of Ibsen is both false and misleading; and a generation of excellent critics, analysts, and biographers have devoted themselves to exposing the injustice and superficiality of such conclusions. Nevertheless, the perception persists in the general mind, and it is usually consolidated in the theatre, on the few occasions when plays by Ibsen are staged. We know that, even at his most apparently prosaic, Ibsen remained a great poet, but the Ibsen who is most immediately recognized by the public is a crude psychologist of the conscious mind, and a clumsy set designer who tries to create living spaces out of canvas and glue, with doors that wiggle on their frames, and windows that look out on painted views of fjords. Ibsen could not have foreseen the advent of motion pictures, though he does tantalize us, in *The Wild Duck,* over some revolutionary invention in photography that Hjalmar Ekdal pretends to be working on. But the movies have had the effect of rendering many of Ibsen's stage devices unworkable. For it can be argued that the theatre is no longer able to compete with the film medium in creating a realistic environment. We are much too familiar with close-up reality now to be charmed by theatrical simulations, no matter how much verisimilitude the designer can devise. After the authentic locations seen on the screen, it is unlikely that fake environments of the stage can persuade us, any longer, to suspend our disbelief, no matter how artfully they may be constructed.

By the same token, those middle-class men and women whom Frank Wedekind contemptuously called *Haustier*—continually turning gas lamps on and off to suggest their enlightened or benighted states—are now as recognizable to us as our own brothers and sisters, but, alas, as predictable too. Instead of astonishing us, as they astonished Ibsen's contemporaries, instead of appearing as a new stage species, they are now all too familiar from continual repetition in countless post-Ibsen plays; and Ibsen, the enemy of all that is conventional, is ironically suffering the fate of being identified with the conventional, of being held accountable for much that is stale and stodgy on our contemporary stage. The theatrical revolution that Ibsen helped to initiate has been so successful that today it informs our establishment acting-training, directing techniques, and design strategies, which now constitute the conventional modes against which a new breed of theatrical revolutionaries are defining themselves. Brecht, who once declared Ibsen obsolete, said it was the theatre artist's obligation to make the familiar strange, and the strange familiar; after Brecht, it soon became common to charge Ibsen with encouraging the familiar onstage, and not only the familiar, but the safe, the comfortable, the culinary.

Those of us in the theatre who love Ibsen, therefore, have an obligation to rescue him from such misapprehensions and misconceptions, first by rediscovering the heroic dimension of Ibsen's characters, and secondly, by excavating the poem that always lies half-buried in Ibsen's prose mechanisms. We know that even toward the end of his career, Ibsen always claimed to have remained a poet, not a social thinker; we are also aware that he always created his work out of a powerful and textured poetic imagination, even though he made a conscious, painful decision to dispense with verse. As he told Lucie Wolf in a famous letter, "During the last seven or eight years, I have hardly written a single verse, devoting myself exclusively to the very much more difficult art of writing the straightforward, plain language spoken in daily life." What he didn't say was that this language only *seemed* plain and straightforward, that it was pulsing with ambiguity, and that, underneath the deceptively simple surface, lay an elusive nexus of images, symbols, and metaphors.

That hidden poetry is the reality of Ibsen, not the illusion of surfaces. And it is the duty of directors, actors, and designers alike, at this moment in theatrical history, to explore that poetic reality, even if this means rejecting physical verisimilitude altogether. For if it is the poet's task to *see,* then nothing has prevented us from seeing what Ibsen saw more than the clumsy machinery of realism that informs his plays both in the study and on the stage. It is our duty to explore the visionary side of Ibsen by looking below the comfortable and familiar images of everyday life. The place to find this visionary quality is in the text itself, for that is where Ibsen hid it. Anyone who has ever worked carefully on an Ibsen play, either for the sake of analyzing, teaching, or directing it, knows that everything is there for a purpose, including a complicated apparatus of clues and hints about his interior meanings. What is true of Shakespeare is just as true of Ibsen—namely, that a thorough understanding of the text will always yield a fresh and original interpretation, just as a stale production is always the result of superficial reading and received ideas.

Let me frame my remarks in the form of an exhortation to future Ibsen directors and readers: Find the poem inside the play, and you will have found the play. And permit me to advise all future Ibsen actors to imagine they are performing not in *All My Sons* and *The Hot l Baltimore,* but rather in *Othello* and *King Lear.* For characters in Ibsen owe more to Shakespeare than they do to Hebbel or Scribe; they are heroic creations, despite their bourgeois origins. The spirit of Brand lives in Gregers Werle, just as the spirit of Peer Gynt lives in Hjalmar Ekdal; the Vikings and trolls of Ibsen's earlier drama lurk behind every door and window of *The Wild Duck* and *The Master Builder.* What is buttoned-up and commonplace about the characters of Ibsen's modern plays is not what they are, but rather what they have been forced to become; and it is this banalizing condition of modern life that constitutes Ibsen's central theme. In developing an Ibsen character, the modern actor must show us both what the character is and what he might have been, the essential creature of nature and how this natural creature has been forced to adapt for the sake of survival in society.

I am suggesting, in other words, that Ibsen, like every great writer, must be rediscovered by every new generation, and this means going beyond what is known to what is still there to be unearthed. But there is another great area of rediscovery for Americans, and that is the nature of Ibsenism itself. By this I mean the content of Ibsen's thought, insofar as that can be gleaned from his letters, speeches, and plays.

I am, of course, well aware that Ibsen himself was always afraid of being institutionalized, and that the ideology called Ibsenism, as defined by such well-intentioned followers as Bernard Shaw, is hardly a satisfactory way to approach a complicated artist, no matter how valuable it might have been in defining Bernard Shaw. As we know, Ibsen always thought himself, with considerable justice, to be moving away from any fixed position, engaged as he was in a continual process of intellectual and creative evolution that made it impossible for anyone to establish a quintessence of Ibsenism. "I maintain," he wrote in a letter to Georg Brandes, "that a fighter in the intellectual vanguard cannot possibly gather a majority around him. . . . The majority, the mass, the mob will never catch up with him, and he can never have the majority with him. As regards myself at least, I am quite aware of such unceasing progress. At the point where I stood when I wrote each of my books there now stands a tolerably compact crowd; but I myself am no longer there. I am elsewhere; farther ahead, I hope."

Well, here we stand, all of us, a tolerably compact crowd around each of Ibsen's books; and he still stands elsewhere, considerably farther ahead. And none of us would have it otherwise, for if we ever assimilate Ibsen, if we ever "understand" him completely, then he will have become a domesticated animal, too, having lost that untamed, evasive quality that attracted us to him in the first place. Still, I do believe it is possible to catch this wild bird in flight, just for a moment as in a freeze frame—not to define his dogma, since he possessed none, but rather to identify the posture with which he gracefully avoided being fixed in dogma. It is this posture that, with some hesitation, I would call Ibsenism; and it is this posture which keeps him engaged in his "unceasing progress," always farther ahead than the tolerably compact crowd.

The task is necessary, I believe, because Ibsenism has still failed to leave its mark on us. It is a remarkable fact, considering Ibsen's fame, that for all the influence he has had on the social and intellectual life of Americans, he might just as well have never written a word. If you doubt this, just think of what he would have said, had he had the opportunity to observe our mores and behavior as he once observed those of his own countrymen. What would Ibsen have said, for example, of a nation dedicated to forcing democracy into every area of endeavor except the one for which it was originally designed, namely, political and economic equality? What would he have thought about our intellectual life, where scholars popularize their learning and critics swallow their standards to reach a wider market? How would he have regarded our educational system, which has installed mediocrity as a national norm in the face of pressures from administrators, students, and parents alike? What would he have said about our obsessive concern for material comforts and our sacrifice of the spirit? How would he have regarded the way we manipulate language to alter reality and retouch the truth? With what scorn would he have greeted the loss of individualism in our society, and the way in which majority and minority groups coerce dissenting opinion? What would he have said of our liberal press, our conservative politics, our Watergates and Vietnams, our commodity theatre, our system of rewards and prizes, our corporate-controlled media, our industrial poisons, our endless daily conflicts between men and women, parents and children, blacks and whites, employers and unions, gays and straights, Jews and Gentiles, city-dwellers and farmers?

We already know what Ibsen would say because he has said it; and the fact that he said it so well, and that we have not heard it, is bound to create a little disenchantment with the idea of human progress. Yet perhaps it might be valuable to listen to Ibsen on these subjects again, if only to demonstrate the remarkable cogency and prescience with which he analyzed our problems, a hundred years before we were in a position to suffer them.

Among the major political issues being debated today is the responsibility of the individual to the state, for involved in this issue is the whole question of equal rights, not to mention the relationship between the artist and the citizen, and how much private freedom should be sacrificed to the needs of the larger group. This is one of the things Ibsen had to say (in a letter to Brandes) about the whole political process. "As to liberty, I take it that our disagreement is a disagreement about words. I shall never agree to making liberty synonymous with political liberty. What you call liberty, I call liberties; and what I call the struggle for liberty is nothing but the steady, vital growth and pursuit of the very conception of liberty. He who possesses liberty as something already achieved possesses it dead and soulless; for the essence of the idea of liberty is that it continue to develop steadily as men pursue it and make it part of their being. Anyone who stops in the middle and says, 'Now I have it,' shows that he has lost it. It is exactly this tendency to stop dead when a certain amount of liberty has been acquired that is characteristic of the political state—and it is this that I said was not good. Of course it is a benefit to possess the right to vote, the right of self-taxation, etc. But who benefits? The citizen, not the individual. Now there is absolutely no logical necessity for the individual to become a citizen. On the contrary [his favorite phrase], the state is the curse of the individual. . . . The state must be abolished! In that revolution I will take part. Undermine the idea of the state; make willingness and spiritual kinship the only essentials for union—and you have the beginning of a liberty that is of some value. Changing one form of government for another is merely a matter of toying with various degrees of the same thing—a little more or a little less. Folly, all of it. Yes, dear friend, the great thing is not to allow oneself to be frightened by the venerableness of institutions. The state has its roots in time; it will reach its height in time."

I have quoted at such length from this letter because it contains, I think, the taproot of Ibsenism, and its appropriateness to our time; just consider Ibsen's remarks in relation to that most pressing contemporary American issue, feminism and women's rights. Ibsen has been expropriated by the women's movement—today, as in his own era—as an ally in the fight for female liberation, because of such plays as *A Doll's House* and *Lady from the Sea,* but such specific designations always confused him, given his concern for humankind in general. Addressing the Norwegian League for Women's Rights, he had this to say: "I am not a member of the Women's Rights League. Whatever I have written has been written without any conscious thought of making propaganda. I have been more the poet and less the social philosopher than people generally seem inclined to believe. I thank you for the toast, but must disclaim the honor of having consciously worked for the women's rights movement. I am not even quite clear as to just what this women's rights movement really is. To me it has seemed a problem of mankind in general. . . . True enough, it is desirable to solve the woman problem, along with all the others; but that has not been the whole purpose. My task has been the *description of humanity.* "

This is the answer Ibsen gave to every group that tried to expropriate him for its cause: "My task has been the description of humanity." Even more, he might have said, "My task has been the description of the *struggle* of humanity," for it was the sense of continuing struggle, of process, of movement, of change that obsessed him, rather than the accumulation and consolidation of special liberties for special-interest groups. "All development hitherto has been nothing more than a stumbling from one mistake into another," he wrote. "But the struggle itself is good, wholesome, invigorating." Or as his hero, Brand, discovered, "Man must struggle till he dies"—it is the struggle, not the goal, that mattered most. Why so much emphasis on struggle? Because that is what keeps the human animal alive. It was the struggle against both external and internal enemies—the forces in society that would tame and domesticate you, and the forces in the self that would have you settle for half. "What I recommend for you," he advised Brandes, "is a thorough-going, full-blooded egoism. . . . There is no way you can benefit society more than by coining the metal you have in yourself."

By egoism, Ibsen did not mean narcissism, which is how we have translated his meaning into our own self-indulgent tongue. He recognized that there was an artist or genius in every self which was almost another self—another persona within us—to be nurtured and cared for, as we would nurture and care for a child. He meant that the writer's talent was not there to advance the writer; it was a means to advance the writer's art. He meant that the actor's gifts were designed not for preening and strutting, but rather for the service of something higher than the attainment of celebrity. Self-realization, not self-promotion; loving the art in yourself rather than yourself in art. "I have been a poor caretaker of my talent," Scott Fitzgerald complained toward the end of his life. Ibsen's demand on us was that we be good caretakers of our talent, for this talent was a loan or gift that we held without possessing, something we could either develop or destroy.

A thorough-going, full-blooded egoism, then, did not mean creating an Empire of Self, as Peer Gynt learned to his regret; one discovered the self only by slaying the self. What Ibsen is describing is the development of moral character through the exercise of the will. This sort of thing admittedly falls strangely on the ears of our time, but it is the essential component of Ibsenism, and the basis for the only kind of human supremacy that Ibsen recognized. For Ibsen did not believe that anyone could lay claim to superiority in consequence of being male or female, black or white, rich or poor, or even on the basis of inherited gifts. The aristocracy he called for was an aristocracy of character, will, and spirit; the nobility he described was a natural nobility that transcended class and inheritance, that distinguished the individual from the state, and the artist from the citizen.

For Ibsen believed that the artist and the political animal were unalterably opposed, indeed, were incapable of occupying the same space. "For every statesman who crops up there," he wrote, "an artist will be ruined. And the glorious longing for liberty—that is at an end now. Yes—I for one must confess that the only thing I love about liberty is the struggle for it; I care nothing for the possession of it. . . . How the old ideas will come tumbling about our ears! And high time they did. Up till now we have been living on nothing but crumbs from the revolutionary table of the last century, and I think we have been chewing on that stuff long enough. The old terms must be reinvested with new meaning, and given new explanations. Liberty, Equality, and Fraternity are no longer what they were in the days of the late-lamented guillotine. That is what politicians will not understand; and that is why I hate them. They want only their own special revolutions—external revolutions, political revolutions, etc. But that is only dabbling. What is really needed is a revolution of the human spirit."

A revolution of the human spirit! With this, Ibsen makes his break with contemporary materialistic thought, and reveals his secret messianic ambitions. For Ibsen conceived his own mission to be a spiritual one, his role as an artist to provide the modern religion that would replace the worn-out creeds of Caesarism and Christianity, of the secular state and the spiritual hierarchy. This ambition—dramatized in *Brand* and codified in *Emperor and Galilean*—explains Ibsen's indifference to political revolution and social advance, for it was to be realized through culture, art, and education. As Ibsen conceived his "Third Empire," it was to be a synthesis of Roman self-assertion and Christian self-abnegation; today, it looks to us more like an extension of Protestantism, with its demand that each man be his own church, even his own God. But as always with Ibsen, the end result was less important than the struggle toward that end, the actual content of his messianic doctrine of less significance than the process through which it was to be achieved.

And more important than both was the perception that inspired them: Ibsen's belief that what is commonly called progress is simply a disguised form of further disintegration that will eventually leave us stranded on the shoals of false ideals. "There are actually moments," he wrote, "when the whole history of the world reminds one of a sinking ship; the only thing to do is save oneself. Nothing will come of special reforms. The whole human race is on the wrong track." The passage reverberates with Doctor Stockmann's discovery that "he is the strongest who stands alone," and reminds us that, however honored and bemedaled Ibsen became toward the conclusion of his career, for most of his life he stood alone. Having chosen exile, he suffered for it, with a crushing loneliness and sense of alienation, as he confided to a group of university students bent on paying him homage: "He who wins a home for himself in foreign lands—in his inmost soul he scarcely feels at home anywhere—even in the country of his birth." But such was his temperament that he also found such isolation bracing. The advice he gives to Brandes, suffering a similar kind of ostracism, shows the posture he has adopted for himself. "You say that every voice in the faculty of philosophy is against you. Dear Brandes, how else would you want it: Are you not fighting against the philosophy of the faculty? . . . If they did not lock you out, it would show they are not afraid of you . . . To me your revolt is a great, emancipating outbreak of genius. . . . I hear you have organized a society. Do not rely implicitly upon everyone who joins you. With an adherent, everything depends upon the reasons for his adherence. Whether you may be strengthening your position or not, I cannot tell. To me it appears that the man who stands alone is the strongest."

How strangely, how chillingly such words fall upon the ears of twentieth-century America, where the terror of aloneness is so pervasive that a whole technology has been devised to defend us against a single moment of solitude. What does Ibsen have to communicate to a people who, if they desire a transcendent life at all, seek it at mass rallies in Yankee Stadium, or in the spiritual barbiturates of the Reverend Moon and the Mahatma Ji, or in the totalitarian seances of *est* and encounter sessions. How does an intelligent student stand alone against the passionate collectivity of the young? How does an independent black stand alone against the racial orthodoxies of Black Power? How does a clear-headed woman stand alone against the remorseless sexual categorizing of Women's Liberation? How does an American Jew stand alone against the narrow stances of nationalistic Jewish groups? How does an American novelist establish his independence of the National Book Association, or an American actor of Equity, or an American trucker of the Teamsters' Union? How does a member of the philosophy faculty declare his opposition to the philosophy of the faculty? How does a conservationist express his conviction that the air and oceans are being poisoned in the face of expensive promotional campaigns by wealthy industrial corporations? And finally, how does a solitary American preserve his autonomy within a government of agencies devoted to manipulating and controlling his destiny?

Clearly, the United States today is a massive conglomerate of pressure groups and political lobbies and liberation fronts and committees—a huge magnetic force which yanks every particle into its orbit—where nothing can be heard or accomplished until it is first monitored, scanned, blipped, and X-rayed by a vast bureaucratic mechanism. For those who no longer find Ibsen's choice of exile possible, the remaining options are silence and cunning, or conformity, or the gradual obliteration of the moral will by the mad intellect of democracy.

The impact of Ibsenism on our time, then, has been minimal, and Ibsen's skepticism about progress is daily being confirmed. Along with many of the other major thinkers of his century—Nietzsche and Kierkegaard and Emerson, for example—and many of those of ours—such as Freud and Santayana and Ortega y Gasset—he has been drowned out by a clamorous chorus of self-interested collectives, bent on shaping all art and thought to their own specific prejudices. But Ibsen foresaw even this, and he gave us both the means to combat it and the courage to confront it when he told the guests at a Stockholm banquet: "It has been said of me on different occasions that I am a pessimist. And so I am insofar as I do not believe in the everlastingness of human ideals. But I am also an optimist insofar as I firmly believe in the capacity for the propagation and development of ideals. . . . Therefore, permit

me to drink a toast to the future—to that which is to come."
Let us, who honor Ibsen, offer a toast to this seminal intellect,
this prodigious artist, this prodigal individual. For by honor-
ing him in our own bad times, we keep faith with the future as
well.

(1978)

FIVE

The Theatre Audience: A House Divided

WHENEVER PEOPLE speak to me of the need for an American national theatre, I generally reply that we cannot have a national theatre unless we have a nation. Contemporary America constitutes not one but many nations, each with its own political ambitions, its own language, gestures, and symbols, its own hunger for cultural recognition. How can a single theatre hope to develop a body of plays and productions that transcend these national divisions and appeal to a general American public?

This question was raised to mind again during the visit of our Yale Repertory Theatre to New York City in the summer of 1978. In June, we brought two works to Joseph Papp's Public Theatre—Andrei Serban's production of Molière's *Sganarelle* and Arthur Kopit's new play, *Wings.* During the four weeks we were in residence at the Newman Theatre, a number of productions came and went at the other Public Theatre stages, including a feminist musical, a one-man Artaud show, a one-woman evening of poetry and music, and two one-act black plays. Each of these productions attracted its own special audience, and each of these audiences seemed entirely independent, if not somewhat wary, of the others.

For our own productions, the audiences were large and appreciative, but I could not help noticing that they were significantly different from the other audiences at the Public, indeed, different from audiences traditionally associated with New York. It struck me, then, that—subtly, gradually, inexorably—the audience for theatre has been changing in the last few years, a transformation that is now evident not only at the Public, but, to a lesser degree, in the American theatre at large. Even on Broadway, where the appeal is assumed to be more popular and general, the audiences have grown relatively compartmentalized: mostly black audiences for *The Mighty Gents* and *The Wiz,* tourist audiences for the comedies and musicals, and for *Gemini* and *Dracula* what Broadway actors call "bridge and tunnel" audiences, meaning essentially blue- and white-collar people from New Jersey and Long Island.

Where was the serious, theatrically sophisticated audience that once supported the more ambitious New York plays? Not, apparently, at our productions of *Sganarelle* and *Wings.* It's always dangerous to generalize about large groups of people, but we had the sense that many of our audience members were drawn there by favorable reviews rather than by any interest in Molière and Kopit, and often, therefore, seemed in some initial doubt about how to receive our work. No matter how enthusiastic they became by the end of the evening, these audiences—unlike others we saw at the Public—did not initially receive our plays as extensions of their own lives and culture, and as a result, they often failed to enter the productions as true spectators until twenty or thirty minutes into the evening.

I thought to myself at the time that the most suitable New York Public Theatre audience for *Sganarelle* (a collection of classic French farces) would have been a coterie of expatriated seventeenth-century Frenchmen, while the more appropriate audience for *Wings* (a play about a stroke victim) would have been a hospital ward of aphasiacs. The people there were simply not accustomed to making an imaginative leap into something they did not recognize as part of their immediate world. Admittedly, the audiences Joseph Papp has been developing over the years on Lafayette Street are special, but it cannot be denied that they typify something as well: a radical change in American society, over the past fifteen or twenty years, that has resulted in the Balkanization of our entire theatre culture.

This is not to say that the social developments of recent times have been unproductive in the theatre. Unquestionably —as Mr. Papp's work continually demonstrates—the rise of the black movement, the movement for women's rights, the gay liberation movement, and countless other such challenges to the status quo have been responsible for stimulating talent and inspiring activity in areas that were previously untapped. One no longer needs to describe the achievements that have issued from our increased racial, sexual, and ethnic awareness. If it has accomplished nothing else, this new consciousness has freed us forever from the danger of conformity to a single homogenized national character.

Still, if the rejection of the melting-pot ethos by various American minorities has contributed a rich diversity to culture and has advanced the standing of certain disadvantaged groups, it has also resulted in the loss of something valuable, namely, our unity as a nation and our capacity to create universal works of art. The theatre can certainly be used as an instrument for raising consciousness, or evacuating rage, or stimulating pride, but it has another, older function as the locus of a shared experience, a compound of everything that has been imagined, learned, and dreamed. This is what usually seems to be missing from our stage these days—not the sense of what it means to be black or gay or a woman in 1978, but of what it means to be an American in this century, if not a human being in this millennium. When Eugene O'Neill wrote about an Irish family living in New London in the early decades of the century, he was concerned both with what made the Tyrones special and with what united them to other families in history, just as Richard Wright, in *Native Son,* told us as much about crime and punishment as he did about the agony of being black in Southern society.

Martin Luther King used to say that he was less interested in the future of black people than he was in the future of America; it was just that America's future happened to be intimately bound up with the resolution of the black problem. This majestic insight could only have proceeded from a unifying imagination. With the rise of the Black Power movement following King's assassination, the emphasis of the country changed from integration to separatism, and King's grand sense of the American destiny was consequently abandoned. The separatist impulse now seems to dominate dozens of special-interest groups, each trying to elbow the other aside for power and influence, and we have become a nation of political lobbies instead of a people, dissipating vital creative energies in the formulation of petitions and propaganda.

At the same time, our culture is in the process of becoming an extension of our politics—which may be the only significant legacy that the 1960s, with its emphasis on the politicized consciousness, has left to us. Instead of a national community in whose embrace we are all enfolded, we have broken into a multifaceted complex of isolated constituencies, each with its own advocates and publicists, each arguing for moral, social, and aesthetic supremacy; meanwhile, our artists and artistic institutions spend their time competing for the attention of the media, the funds of the government, the admiration of the public. Designed as a federation of separate states, our country has historically tended to divide into political and cultural units, Abraham Lincoln's mighty attempt to preserve the "Union" being only one of the continuing efforts by statesmen to resolve these contentions and bring the nation together. But whereas American politics, in the past, might have featured a conflict between large forces like North and South, and American culture divided between high and popular art, today we have splintered into so many fragments that the shape of the country is now almost indeterminate.

And the shape of our theatre has suffered accordingly. In New York, for example, one can find virtually every variety of play imaginable, performed in every kind of theatre for every kind of spectator; what one cannot find is the center that unifies these disparate elements—a major resident company performing the great classical works in combination with significant American plays. On Broadway, where musicals, light comedies, and successful transfers from nonprofit theatres are the common staples, there has not, to my knowledge, been a classical production originated by American actors under commercial management in at least ten years.* At the New York Shakespeare Festival in Central Park, Mr. Papp continues to do Shakespeare and other classics during the summer months, in innovative productions with racially integrated companies (though even his Park audiences seem limited to particular classes and ages); but at the Public during the winter, he usually prefers to develop special projects, appealing to special audiences, often featuring racially, sexually, or ethnically determined casts (the most recent being a black and Hispanic company preparing two Shakespeare plays). Frank Dunlop has recently attempted to produce classical plays at the Brooklyn Academy of Music with an American company of actors; but Mr. Dunlop is British, his efforts were seasonal, and the theatre seems to attract mainly people from the neighbor-

---

*Al Pacino's *Richard III* became an exception in 1979.

hood.* Circle in the Square usually includes a classic in its season (for example, *The Inspector General* and *Man and Superman*), but it mainly concentrates on revivals of recent American plays. The Vivian Beaumont Theatre at Lincoln Center is the only theatre in New York specifically designed for the classical repertory. Significantly enough, it has been dark for some time, ever since Mr. Papp—the fourth managerial casualty of that ill-fated venture—relinquished his directorship.

The history of the Beaumont, as a matter of fact, offers an interesting historical perspective on the fate of the serious general audience in New York. The first management, presided over by Robert Whitehead and Elia Kazan, apparently assumed that the audience for a repertory theatre was similar to that of Broadway and, as a result, offered plays that were indistinguishable from those they had been producing in the commercial theatre: two plays by Arthur Miller, a revival of an O'Neill, and a light comedy by S. N. Behrman. When they later attempted, and badly mauled, their first classical production—*The Changeling,* directed by Mr. Kazan—they lost their audience *and* their theatre. The next management, under Herbert Blau and Jules Irving, was recruited from the embryonic resident theatre movement, namely from the Actors Workshop in San Francisco; but (perhaps because the movement was *too* embryonic then) the imaginative play selection was not supported by equally imaginative production, and Mr. Blau resigned before he was able to build a company or train an audience for classical theatre. With Mr. Irving remaining in charge, the Beaumont became something of a caretaker operation, offering anthology plays in conventional productions, thus satisfying an audience that was less interested in seeing a play than in being seen at one.

It was this audience that the irrepressible Joseph Papp attempted to transform when he, rather reluctantly, took on the

---

*Dunlop's replacement, David Jones, is also British, and his plans for the repertory are very similar (1979).

responsibilities of the Beaumont. Mr. Papp's heart—not to mention his office and his staff—remained downtown on Lafayette Street, and as a result, he initially decided to provide the Beaumont audiences with the same kind of fare that had been successful at the Public Theatre—"hunchback" American plays (as he called them) in sequential performances with self-contained casts. When the audiences, along with the critics, rejected most of these plays, Mr. Papp (still not prepared to form a permanent company) then turned to a series of contemporary classics, including *A Doll's House* and *Mrs. Warren's Profession,* featuring national and international stars. This kind of glitter was obviously more to the taste of the Beaumont audience, but it was just as obviously not to the taste of Mr. Papp, who, in his final season, changed his policy once again, producing a group of transformed classics, directed by Andrei Serban and Richard Foreman, two young artists who had distinguished themselves doing experimental work on the off-off-Broadway stage.

These innovative productions—*The Threepenny Opera, The Cherry Orchard,* and Aeschylus' *Agamemnon*—were each in their way genuinely exciting and controversial productions. But while they generally excited most of the New York critics, and generally engaged the Beaumont audience, Mr. Papp announced his decision to relinquish Lincoln Center and return full time to his downtown operations, just at the point when he seemed to be breaking the Lincoln Center jinx. Mr. Papp's decision was primarily made for economic reasons. The Beaumont was draining the profits of *A Chorus Line* (the main source of his funding) so quickly that it threatened to exhaust his resources in two years. But his decision had a philosophical basis as well—he simply did not enjoy producing this kind of theatre. The constant policy changes he announced and introduced as director suggest that he was always restless in his role at the Beaumont, and he never bothered to disguise the faint air of disdain with which he regarded the Beaumont audience.

Joseph Papp and New York are virtually identical, and it may be that his present mode of operation—experimenting with specific audiences of distinctly different characters—is the most sensible approach to New York theatre at the present time. But it leaves New York without a major repertory company and without a serious general audience. It also leaves our country without even the pretense of a national theatre. To accept such a condition is to accept our present state as a nation of splinter groups, and to condone the current tendency to cluster into isolated enclaves of special interests with nothing to say to each other.

It is often justly charged, by myself among others, that the "general audience" to which I have been referring is essentially white, middle-class, middle-aged, and establishment; this has certainly been the make-up of the audience at the Beaumont in recent years. But the general audience is also potentially a cross-section of all the classes, races, ages, and ethnic groups in the country. The common denominator that might unite these divided groups is not a theatrical appeal based on their own lives and expectations, since few in this country share the same lives and expectations, but rather a dramatic appeal based on their imaginations and dreams, which virtually everybody has in common. (Lower ticket prices and a more relaxed theatrical environment would also be of help.) In England, the plays of Shakespeare provide a common cultural resource for the people; in France, it is the plays of Molière; in Scandinavia, the plays of Ibsen and Strindberg; in the Soviet Union, the plays of Chekhov. With the possible exception of Eugene O'Neill in his later years, a universal genius has not yet been developed in America who encapsulates, and thereby unites, the history and culture of a whole people.

Perhaps we will never develop this genius, by reason of our heterogeneous social character, but this doesn't mean we should stop trying, any more than we should stop trying to heal our divisions and discover our common bonds. Whitman said that great poets need great audiences. It may be that great audiences help to *make* great poets. If we can find some way to form a general American audience, then we may not only have a universal artist and a national theatre, we may even have our country whole again.

(1978)

PART IV

LEISURE
MOMENTS:
Satires, Stories, Plays

CONTENTS

ONE

Oedipus Nix: A Mythical Tragedy (from Watergate Classics)

OEDIPUS Children, citizens of Thebes, why do you come before me while the city smokes with shrieks and leaks and lamentations? Do you know anything that I can do and have not done?

CHORUS OF THE SKEPTICS Oedipus, King of our country, we all stand here because the city stumbles toward disaster, hardly able to hold up its head. A blight has fallen upon us —corruption ravages the state. And there are those who say you know the cause.

CHORUS OF THE MIDDLE Oedipus, not God but foremost among upright men, seeing that when you first came to Thebes, you exposed the uncleanness of your adversaries, muzzled your enemies, and imprisoned those who spat upon our wars, we beseech you to find some help. Uplift our state. Think upon your fame which you have ever kept as clean as tooth of hound. Remember that it is better to rule over men than over a waste place.

OEDIPUS   My unhappy children! I know well what suffering
you endure; yet sufferers though you be, there is not a single
one whose suffering is as mine—each mourns himself, but
my soul mourns the city, myself, and you. I have sweat many
lip-drops and searched hither and thither for some remedy.
And though I have said, each man must learn to help himself, yet will I help you. I have this day appointed Creon, the
most upright man in the realm, to visit the Delphic Oracle,
and tell if any word or deed of mine may yet deliver the
town.

CREON   Good news: for pain turns to pleasure when we have
set the crooked straight. Our lord Apollo says we must root
out the evil that is polluting the state or perish. He bids us
purify ourselves by driving out a defiling thing that has been
cherished in this land.

OEDIPUS   What thing is that?

CREON   Know you not that in your early reign, men broke the
locks upon your adversaries' doors, stole forth their papers,
and overheard their private conversations?

OEDIPUS   I heard of that, and soon declared not one among
my courtiers, presently employed, had aught to do with that
bizarre occurrence.

CREON   The Oracle says that people of your court both did
the deed and did conceal it, and now demands we find the
culprits, whoever they may be.

OEDIPUS   Then let me make a thing perfectly clear: Neither
did I participate in such a deed nor have any knowledge of
its origins. So whoever among you knows by what men these
deeds were done must tell all he knows. And if a man keep
silent from fear or to screen a friend, he shall be driven to
the judges as if he himself were guilty. I pray the corrupter's

life be cursed, whether he did the deed with others or by himself alone, whether of my court or of my adversaries' party. There can be no whitewash of the palace of Thebes.

MIDDLE CHORUS   If there be such a man, and terror can move him, he will not keep silent when they have told him of your curses.

OEDIPUS   Yet hear me while I make but one thing clearer: None who entered conversation with me should reveal our private speech, and if he does, I pray that his life be accursed as well, for our high secrets cannot be exposed to public eyes.

SKEPTIC CHORUS   If there be such a man, and terror can move him, then he *must* keep silent when they have told him of your curses.

OEDIPUS   Not so, children of Thebes. The privilege of executives is holy in all things touching on security. Our secrets have been leaking through the streets, and I must stop the holes before the city sinks. But know you clearly one important thing: I seek to find the truth whoever is involved. And should the criminal prove close to me, he too must suffer for his guilt, and I will take responsibility, though not the blame.
   (Exit)

MIDDLE CHORUS   The King remains alone within his palace, or spends his weekends on Parnassus musing. Now men plead guilty and do not speak, and others tell of stranger kinds of crimes. Each points his finger at a friend, while accusations buzz like insects in our ears.

SKEPTIC CHORUS   Each day, another revelation smites the land, while corruption rises high in every nostril. But some there are who still can pierce the shrouds of doubt. And here comes one, the blind prophet, Tiresias, who shall set the crooked straight, in whom alone of all men the truth lies.

OEDIPUS *(Entering)* Tiresias, the plague is among us, and from that plague, Great Prophet, some say you can protect and save us.

TIRESIAS Let me go home. I have no wish to speak. You will bear the burden more easily to the end, and I bear mine, if you but give me leave to go.

OEDIPUS That will I not, for I hear a kind of accusation in your speech. It seems to me that you have helped to plot the deed; and short of doing it with your own hands, have done the deed yourself.

TIRESIAS Make me the scapegoat? Then will I say, *You* are the defiler of the land.

OEDIPUS So brazen in your impudence? How do you hope to escape punishment?

TIRESIAS You have spurred me to speech against my will. But if I must talk, I say that those most close to you have done this deed, and for your sake, to keep you on the throne.

OEDIPUS You shall rue it for having spoken twice such lying words. But, children of Thebes, since this has now been said, clear perfectly must I make one thing at last: If some among my court have done this deed, then they must leave it, heaped with my honors and highest praise. But I was never told of this or much of anything, and did not know or see or hear or feel this deed. Oh, innocence, how helpless you are before the smears of naughty men. Power, ability, position, you must bear all burdens, and yet what envy you create. Great must be that envy if it has made Tiresias secretly long to take that power from me, in union with my adversaries.

JOCASTA Unhappy men! Why have you made this crazy uproar? Are you not ashamed to quarrel when the whole country watches? What put you in this anger?

OEDIPUS   He says that I am guilty of the crime that blights our land.

JOCASTA   My husband, have no fear of what he says. Have you not made peace with honor, and concluded a pact with your former enemies in Corinth and in Sparta? And is not your mandate from the people clear, who crowned you King by sixty-four percent?

OEDIPUS   Dear wife, my true companion in purity and cleanness, who always smiled upon my speeches and never smoked in public places, your speech brings courage to my heart. Hear me, friends, I have a last thing to make perfectly clear: My former statements on this theme are now inoperative. I may have been less vigilant than my wont, preoccupied as I am with heavy things of state. I now return to these most high responsibilities: to enforce the peace with arms and feast the mighty heroes of our wars. My servant, Creon, I hereby name to carry on the search. He shall pursue the criminal with all the instruments of state, and end the plague that festers in our land.
   (*Exit*)

MIDDLE CHORUS
   An ambitious man may lift up a whole state,
   And in his death be blessed, and fortunate in his life.
   Our King made war against our distant enemies
   And settled law and order on the land;
   He placed the sacred meat upon our tables
   And kept bad tidings from our harassed ears;
   Though the wars go on and meat is too expensive,
   Our King is greater than a God.

SKEPTIC CHORUS
   They say that character is destiny:
   And sure, a man becomes a tyrant out of insolence;
   He climbs and climbs, until all people call him great,

He seems upon the summit, and God flings him thence.
For should a man abuse the law
And not be punished for it,
Why should we honor justice, or join the sacred dance?

CREON   News, friends, from Delphi, all now has been discovered. The Oracle has named our King as he who first knew
of this terrible crime, and named him as a man who dealt
unjustly with his adversaries. The King has fed our justice
to ravening wolves, while rich men bought his power with
their gold. The plague that blights our state comes from the
throne, and Oedipus is the defiler of the land.

MIDDLE CHORUS   Why do you tell us this and ruin our peace?
Things were ever thus in Thebes, and always will be so. Tell
us no more, but let us till our land, and watch our progeny
grow rich and fat and full.

SKEPTIC CHORUS   No, Creon, speak, for even fat men need to
feed on justice. When Oedipus cursed the criminal, he
cursed himself. Now let the criminal be banished from the
land.

   (Oedipus enters)

JOCASTA   O, King, the people speak with a divided voice, and
now your mandate falls to thirty-two percent.

OEDIPUS   Now, Creon, stop—have you a face so brazen you
accuse a crowned king to his face?

CREON   Hear what I have to say; I can explain all.

OEDIPUS   One thing you will not explain away—that you are
my enemy.

CREON   No enemy, but a messenger from the Oracle, who
now demands you give to me your documents of state.

OEDIPUS   Have you a face so brazen that you come to my
house, the certain robber of my crown?

CREON   Am I such a fool to hunger after unprofitable honors?
I am no contriver of plots; and in proof of this go to the
Pythian Oracle, and ask if I have truly told what the gods
said.

OEDIPUS   The plotter is at his work, and I must counterplot
headlong, or he will get his ends and I miss mine.

CREON   What would you do then? Drive me from the land?

OEDIPUS   Not so; I do not desire your banishment, but your
resignation.

CREON   It is you who must be banished or resign. Alas! I am
on the edge of dreadful words.

OEDIPUS   And I of hearing—yet hear I *won't*. I shall not be
banished, or resign, though all my court be dragged before
Apollo's throne. Upright I remain, and pure, and also hard-
nosed as the Theban rock. Now must I tough it out, devising
master plans. Here shall I stay, though all of Thebes cry, Go.
For on my reign the city's fate depends, and Oedipus' fame
depends on it as well.

CREON   Do not seek to be the master; you won the mastery but
could not keep it to the end.

OEDIPUS   My wife, if I must go, then watch over my two unhappy daughters, Antigone and Ismene, that have ever
loved their father and his wars.

JOCASTA   They shall be watched, o King, but none shall watch
on me. Upright have I been, and clean, and smiled I have
until my jaws did ache. Yet my husband is disgraced and
mud falls on our house. Now will I sow wild oats, and have
my will: frown when I want, drink Bacchic mead, and smoke
in all the public places.

SKEPTIC AND MIDDLE CHORUSES
Make way for Oedipus. All people said

"That is a fortunate man";
And now what storms are beating on his head.
Send prayers to Apollo, and give thanks
For making all things at last so perfectly clear.

(1973)

TWO

Dick's Last Tape (from Watergate Classics)

DICK   *(Briskly)* Ah!
(He bends over ledger, turns the pages, finds the entry he wants, reads)
"Box . . . thrree . . . spool . . . five."
(He raises his head and stares front)
Spool!
(Pause)
Spooool!
(Happy smile. Pause. Bends over table, starts peering and poking at boxes)
Box . . . thrree . . . three . . . four . . . two . . . nine! Good
God! . . . seven . . . Ah! The little rascal.
(He takes up box and peers at it)
Box thrree . . .
(Lays it on table, opens it and peers at spools inside)
Spool . . .
(He peers at ledger)

. . . five . . .
(Peers at spools)
five . . . five . . . ah! The little scoundrel . . .
(Takes out spool and peers at it)
Spool five.
(Lays it on table, closes box three, puts it back with others, takes up spool)
Box three, spool five.
(Bends over machine, looks up. With relish)
Spoooool!
(Happy smile, bends, loads spool on machine. Rubs his hands)
Ah!
(Peers at ledger, reads entry at foot of page)
"Visit of unexpected guest . . ." Hm . . . "Cancer on the
Presidency . . ."
(Raises his head and stares blankly front. Puzzled)
Cancer on the Presidency?
(Peers at ledger, reads)
"Smears and leaks and innuendoes . . ."
(Pauses. Peers again at ledger)
Slight improvement in sweat glands of lip . . . Hm . . . Nation
can't stand pat.
(He raises his head, stares blankly front. Puzzled)
Can't stand pat?
(Pause. He shrugs his shoulders, peers again at ledger. Reads)
"Farewell to" *(He turns the page)* "Bob and John."
*(He raises his head, broods, bends over machine, switches on and
assumes listening posture; i.e., leaning forward, elbows on table,
hand cupping ear toward machine, face front)*

TAPE DICK *(Strong voice, rather pompous, clearly* DICK's *at a much
earlier time)* Sixty today, sound as a bell, and politically I have
now every reason to believe at the *(Hesitates)* . . . crest of the
wave—or thereabouts. Celebrated the great occasion, as in
recent years, quietly at the White House. Telegrams from all
over, and smiles and congratulations from all my aides. In-

stalled new tape system, birthday present from the *(Chuckle)* Secret Service.

(Knock at the door)

A visitor. A chance to test the system, nondirectional . . .

(Sound of door opening and closing)

Ah, yes, why hello, John and Bob; and how are you, my close friends both, the finest public servants I am privileged to know?

TAPE EHRLICHMAN   Happy Birthday, Mr. President. Bob and I would like to wish you every joy on this great day. Your counsel, John Dean, has asked to see you in the Oval Room; he's been cooling his heels in the outer office for a few days now. Says he has something very important to say to you; but if I were you, I'd get him to write that report we spoke about.

TAPE DICK   Well, tell him to sign in, please. He can be our first mystery guest. Why don't you fellows wait for me outside.

(Sound of door slamming)

Why, hello there, handsome John, I'm glad to see you on this important day for the nation. And how is your lovely wife, Maureen?

TAPE DEAN   She's splendid, Mr. President, as smooth as silk. She asked me to wish you a happy birthday, and to thank you for the fine honeymoon you lent us in the Caribbean. But that's not what I've come to see you about . . . You remember, Mr. President, about the break-in at the Watergate, and the demands that Howard Hunt is making for some—

(DICK switches off, broods, looks at his watch, goes backstage in darkness. Ten seconds. Pop of cork. Ten seconds. Second cork. Ten seconds. Third cork. Ten seconds. Brief burst of quavering song)

DICK   Hail to the Chief, etc.

(Fit of coughing, comes back into light, sits down, wipes his mouth, switches on, resumes his listening position)

TAPE DEAN —money to keep his mouth shut. This thing is escalating, sir. And between all those Cubans that are cooling their heels in the pokey, we'd need about a million dollars to make them hold their guilty pleas.

TAPE DICK That should be no problem.
(DICK switches off, raises his head, stares blankly before him. His lips move in the syllables of "But it would be wrong." Then he speaks it into the mike)

DICK But it would be wrong.
(Switches back; turns on machine; assumes listening position)

TAPE DICK That should be no problem.
(Dick's old voice, quavering)
But it would be wrong . . .

TAPE DEAN . . . on the Presidency, a cancer on the Presidency. I just don't know how long we can continue to cover up the . . .
(DICK switches off. Runs tape forward. Stops. Switches on)

TAPE DICK . . . to reveal his private conversations with an aide or an ambassador. It would violate the rules of confidentiality. No one would ever speak candidly to him again. For the same rules of confidentiality apply to a chief executive as to a priest hearing confession, or a lawyer with his client. And so I have decided to withhold these tapes from the prosecutor and the committee on the basis of executive privilege, even though they clearly attest to my innocence of the charges. I have listened to them, and can tell you tonight that they contain nothing that would in any way support the accusations and smears and innuendoes being made against me.
(Pause)
Here I end this reel.
(Pause)

Box . . . three, spool . . . five. *(Pause)* Perhaps my best years are gone. When I had a chance of being loved. But I wouldn't want them back. Not with the conviction I have now. No, I wouldn't want them back.

(DICK *motionless, staring before him. The tape runs on in silence)*

(1973)

THREE

Abou Ben Oilman (A Poem)

Abou Ben Oilman (may his wells increase)
Awoke one night from a deep dream of peace,
And saw within the moonlight of his room,
Making it rich, and like a desert in bloom—
An angel writing in a book of gold.
Exceeding wealth had made Ben Oilman bold,
And to the presence in the room he said,
      "What writest thou?"—The vision raised its
      head,
And with a glance at Abou's rigs and drills,
Answer'd, "The names of those with land in Beverly
      Hills."
      "And is mine one?" said Abou. "Nay, not so,"
Replied the angel. Abou spoke more low,
But cheerily still; and said, "Who gives two damns,
Write me as one who owns the L.A. Rams."
      The angel wrote, and vanished. The next day

It came again, with OPEC surcharges on a silver tray,
And show'd the names of those who now the world possessed,
And lo! Ben Oilman's name led all the rest.

(1974)

FOUR

No Sound, No Fury: A Review of the Ford-Carter Debate

I'd Rather Be President, a prepared improvisation in one act, with two more performances, on tour. Based on briefing books and translated into the Midwestern and Southern by the principals. Directed by Jim Keraya; setting by Bob Witeman; lighting by Imero Florentino; costumes by various haberdashers; presented by the League of Women Voters. At the Walnut Street Theatre, Philadelphia.

THE INCUMBENT	Gerald R. Ford
THE CHALLENGER	Jimmy Carter
THE REFEREE	Edwin Newman
INTERLOCUTOR NO. 1	Frank Reynolds
INTERLOCUTOR NO. 2	James P. Gannon
INTERLOCUTOR NO. 3	Elizabeth Drew

Philadelphia—The two-man show that opened at the Walnut Street Theatre in Philadelphia last Thursday night was performed behind two lecterns separated by a modern abstract form that vaguely resembled a bomb. Though it is cruel to judge a work that is obviously still in out-of-town tryouts, this may well prove an appropriate symbol of the entire tour.

Considering the state of recent American acting, it would be unfair to compare the featured players of the current revival with their famous predecessors. Still, one cannot help observing that when the show was originally produced in 1858 it had a cast that possessed not only great theatrical skill but intriguing physical presence—the short and rotund Stephen A. Douglas, nicely contrasted with the tall and angular Abraham Lincoln.

Nor can one forget how, in the 1960 revival, the steely gaze and rapid-fire delivery of John F. Kennedy made an overnight star out of one who had previously been a relatively unknown supporting player, while his sensitive costar, Richard M. Nixon, though out-performed, was nevertheless able to demonstrate a unique talent (the envy of actors ever since) for making beads of perspiration materialize, at will, on his upper lip.

One need not be nostalgic about the past in order to be disappointed by the present performance. Attired in almost identical costumes, each of the actors has been carefully trained in the contemporary Method school of low-keyed domestic realism, and each has been well-rehearsed. But neither displayed much ability to overcome the handicap of the opening tableau, which found them stiff and expressionless, as if they were already posing for portraits on Mount Rushmore.

Jimmy Carter, who played The Challenger, was rumored earlier to have had difficulty getting a firm grasp on his characterization (there was some indecision over whether he was to play a devout conservative or a liberal swinger), but I found his portrayal of a compassionate citizen, indignant over the callousness of his opponent and inspirited by the nobility of his countrymen, relatively consistent, even occasionally convincing.

Mr. Ford, playing The Incumbent (a role for which some say he has been miscast), also used one of those regional dialects so popular in American theatre these days, drawling out one-syllable words with a gallant disregard for monotony. In his steady characterization of a plodding, deliberate public servant dedicated to ending something he called "the long national nightmare," Mr. Ford ran the risk of substituting for it a long national nap, since like Mr. Carter he intoned his speeches with all the hypnotic concentration of a sleep therapist.

The evening, in short, lacked passion. And though both actors expressed their disapproval of the "energy crisis," each seemed to be suffering an energy crisis of his own. (It was wise of the producers to forbid us any glimpse of the audience, lest our opinion of the show be influenced by the sight of spectators laid out in the aisles.)

The script is in the process of revision and is generally improvised from night to night, so I will refrain from extended comment on its quality. I will only express puzzlement over why actors would take a perfectly good vehicle which has stood the test of time and update it for the sake of some fashionable contemporary "relevance." Even if you approve of tampering with classics, you would probably agree that the climactic moments of the current production, involving tax reform and veto power, are a far cry from the sensational climaxes of the 1960 version when the audience was brought to its feet over the U-2 incident, the missile gap, and the quality of Mr. Nixon's make-up.

In fact, the only effective innovation of the current production, to my mind, was the inspired twenty-seven-minute play-within-a-play, when both actors stood immobilized in silence, staring stonily ahead, visible only from the waist up—though even this was obviously stolen from the works of Samuel Beckett.

The show has two more previews, after which one of the actors will move it to Washington with a much larger cast. It opens to the general public on Jan. 20, with a guaranteed run of at least four years. If this production represents the best the American theatre can offer nowadays, then a general lethargy may spread from the actors to the audience, and the state of apathy will be the next admitted to the Union.

(1976)

FIVE

Channel Crossing (A Story)

IT WAS BECAUSE of their differences regarding Peter's television habits that the Warrens first began quarreling about their new home. The house was a sturdy two-bedroom, imitation-Tudor dwelling on a secluded private street. Calvin had succeeded in buying it for five thousand dollars below the asking price ("already fearfully low for the neighborhood," he was assured by Marian Mayer, the agent handling the sale), and the university had been characteristically generous in its mortgage allowance. Peter's school was no more than a brisk five-minute walk from the house, across a safe campus area of the Yale Divinity School. Shopping was convenient for Susan, on the mornings that her job at the Child Study Center allowed her the luxury of selecting groceries instead of depending on phone deliveries. And the house came with a considerable amount of equipment, most of it in good condition, including a Frigidaire washing machine and dryer, a Disposall, a Storm King dishwasher, a fifteen-cubic-foot freezer—and a handsome twenty-one-inch cable-connected Zenith console color TV.

The trouble was that the television set had been built solidly into the pickled pine cabinets of the room they had chosen for Peter, and it would have been a desecration, Calvin thought, to destroy all that good carpentry out of deference to an irrational prejudice of Susan's.

They had not even unpacked all the dishes and glassware before the Zenith became a subject of heated family debate.

"I think it's worth a little expense to pull the monster out," Susan told Calvin in the midst of their labors. "I just don't understand how the previous owners could have permitted their children such continual exposure."

"Marian told me they were childless," answered Calvin. (He had closed on the house without meeting the sellers.) "I assume they used that room as a den."

"Well, it's a child's room now," replied Susan. "Please have some feelings on the subject. At age ten, Peter is simply not equipped to handle such temptations—his own TV, sending out a nightly flood of idiocy in living color."

"Television doesn't have to be harmful if it's watched moderately," said Calvin, pausing to examine what he perceived to be a small crack in a crystal wine goblet. "You know, you do tend to be a little extreme in these matters. I believe Peter is capable of obeying family rules . . . if they're reasonable."

"Just how many reports and studies does it take to convince you?" Susan said, her exasperation growing. "There's overwhelming proof that television has a decisive influence on a child's development—more powerful than his school, more than us. Once you've allowed that thing inside the house, you have effectively determined Peter's future."

"Oh, God," replied Calvin. He generally found his wife to be rather apocalyptic in her theories of civilization. "Look, I don't like TV either, but you simply can't hand down edicts banning it entirely from Peter's life. It's part of the fabric of the culture. His friends all watch it. Some of his teachers probably use it for visual aids. Our vocabulary is influenced by it. Let's face it, most television *is* a lot of garbage, but it's a fact of modern life. You'll probably be surprised to hear that the Yale Course of Study Committee is presently considering a proposal for a college seminar in the history of video."

"What makes you think I'd be surprised?" replied Susan, who had a rather low opinion of Calvin's colleagues and their academic fashions.

"This is just blind prejudice," said Calvin, beginning to heat up. "What about *Sesame Street* and *The Electric Company* and all that stuff on Channel 13? You've got to make *some* exceptions."

"I will not allow any TV brainwashing in this house as long as I have some say in the matter. You're a university professor, you're supposed to have some stake in these things—but you'd rather drift with the tide. If you took a position on this, Peter might just begin to develop a little character."

"Peter has plenty of character." Cal was getting testy now. Sensitive to rebukes to himself and his profession, he was especially tender about criticism of his son. "You're certainly not going to improve him by extreme measures."

"No television," Susan said. "The set stays off, or we remove it from the house."

But the next morning, at 3:12 A.M. by the illuminated clock-radio on Calvin's bed table, the television set was on.

Susan heard it first. Waking with a start, disoriented by her new surroundings, she perceived a mumble of confused noises coming from Peter's room which made her think the boy was talking in his sleep. When the voices were mixed with music, she found a soft spot between Calvin's ribs with her elbow, and nudged him awake.

"Get up," she whispered. There was a hint of triumph in her voice. "You'd better start dealing with this right away."

Stumbling sleepily between the half-empty cartons on his bedroom floor, Calvin picked his way in the dark to Peter's room. The first thing he noticed upon entering was a blue flickering light playing around the walls. Then, on the television screen, he saw Tyrone Power, bare to the waist, locked in a passionate embrace with Linda Darnell, against a garish landscape of oranges and greens.

Calvin paused, involuntarily caught up by *The Late Late Show* costume epic he saw featured on the Zenith. His son was fast asleep. The bedcovers were tangled around his legs and a faint ribbon of perspiration had formed on his upper lip. Peter's disobedience was unusual and disturbing, but Calvin, for a few moments, was uncertain whether it was grave enough to interrupt his rest.

Susan obviously thought so. Joining her husband in Peter's room, she switched off the television with a violent gesture, and rudely shook the child to consciousness.

Peter's denials of wrongdoing did not surprise Susan, but Cal thought that the child protested his innocence with just enough conviction to raise some doubts about his guilt.

"You're sure we're not doing him an injustice?" he asked his wife over breakfast the next morning, after Peter, his eyes red and puffy, had gone off sullenly to school.

"What do you think?" replied Susan, cracking the crown of her egg with nervous taps of her spoon. "I don't know what you should be more worried about, his disobedience or his lying. But I hope you're finally convinced there's a problem shaping up here."

Both neglected the morning newspaper in their efforts to fix on a suitable consequence for Peter's misbehavior; their system of punishment contained nothing appropriate to such a major family crime. Spankings were forbidden in this household—and television was already prohibited. Finally, Susan suggested that they expropriate Peter's skateboard until further notice.

When the boy returned from school that afternoon, he went up to his room without a word to either parent, and spent the hours before dinner lying on his bed, staring at the ceiling. "I don't care if he sulks," said Susan, though somewhat uncertainly. "At least you can be sure it won't happen again."

But the next morning, at 4:37 A.M., it did happen again. This time, it was Calvin's turn to wake first; the loud hum vibrating through the walls worked on him like a goad. Throwing the covers from his body, he stalked into Peter's room, pushing open the bedroom door so violently that it struck against the closet. There was no question that the TV set was on, or that Peter was watching it. The only question was precisely *what* Peter was watching. For the glass screen was totally blank, its white surface broken only by occasional dark scratches and intermittent signals. In the bed, Peter was sitting bolt upright, fixed on the screen with an expression as empty as the object he was viewing. Calvin called the boy's name, but he did not respond. Instead, he continued to stare, his eyes wide and unblinking, his mouth partly open, at the blank and humming screen. Something seemed to rise and fall in Calvin's rib cage. His voice was hoarse when he called to Susan, and he cleared his throat with difficulty. "I can't seem to wake Peter. I think he's in some sort of trance."

An extreme shiver ran the course of Peter's body, and his fingers were twitching. There was an odor in the room which Calvin could not identify. Throwing his arms around Peter, as if he could revive him with his own bodily warmth, he finally managed to break his son's concentration on the screen.

It was obvious that Peter at first did not recognize either his surroundings or his parents. Red welts were beginning to form on his face, and when Calvin lifted his pajama top, he could see that Peter's slender torso was covered with blotches. Calvin massaged his son's wrists and ankles, murmuring comforting words in his ear.

When Peter finally gained control of his voice, he was in a panic. "I swear to God, Mommy, I never turned it on. Please believe me! I finished reading my book, like you told me, and went to sleep, and the next thing, you were both in my room, and then . . . I have this awful headache and my arms itch."

"Maybe the set turned itself on," said Susan sternly, after Cal had brought Peter an aspirin and tucked him back in his bed.

"It's not impossible, you know," replied Calvin. "perhaps there's a remote control somewhere in the room. A timer, maybe, that switches the damn thing on at odd hours in the morning. I just don't believe Peter would disobey us two days running."

The next night, Calvin had Peter sleep in his parents' room, next to Susan, while he took Peter's place in the room with the Zenith. Peter's bed was too small for Cal; he lay awake, his legs dangling over the bedside, listening to the bells of the Divinity School clock toll the passing hours. He was keeping vigil on a television set.

Cal suppressed a grin. He had been married twelve years, and nothing more serious or ominous than this had ever happened to him. Since he had a strong bond with an intelligent and cultured woman, a tender, imaginative son, a successful career, culminating in a full professorship of comparative literature before he had turned forty, he anticipated a serene, productive future as well. Cal had secret ambitions to conclude his career as president of a small college, or failing that, to take the position that was waiting for him in the foundation his father had worked for. One of his books—a study of the little-known emotional and neurotic side of the rationalist philosopher Descartes—had received enough notice to earn him a position as associate editor on a journal of comparative literature; and his teaching was attracting the attention of serious graduate students. He liked his family a lot and his work well enough. He found life in New Haven to be generally free of the pressures of larger Eastern cities, if a little provincial and isolated. He had, he reflected, discovered a placid alternative to the hectic, brutalizing round of daily existence experienced by most of his friends and college classmates. He was living in America, but America had not happened to him.

He had apparently slipped below the borders of consciousness during these ruminations, because he suddenly found himself being jerked into wakefulness by the sounds of conversation. The numbers on his digital clock (he had brought it with him to Peter's room) read 2:27—but this was not the only illumination in the room. He observed, with a sense of dread, that the television set was on: Directly in his line of vision, a woman he recognized as Gloria Steinem was being interviewed by a heavyset man she called "Joe" about *Ms.* magazine. Against his will, he found his attention held by the hint of malice in "Joe's" questions and the impassive disdain of Steinem's replies. He approached the set, less bewildered now than happy at having established Peter's innocence. He bent to press the button that would turn off the TV; it merely increased the volume. He pressed it again; it improved the picture. He stared at the screen in frustration. Did he smell something burning?

He turned on the overhead light, bent to find the electric plug that brought power to the screen—without success. Apparently, it had been connected to an outlet behind the cabinet. The volume of the TV was beginning to annoy him now, and he could hear his wife and son awakening in confusion in the next room. He turned the volume knob and instantly felt a shock course up his fingers to his arm. After this subsided, he noticed a stinging sensation on his forehead, another on his left arm. An angry welt had formed above his knuckles. He surveyed it solemnly. The smell was stronger now. He identified it as burning wires . . . also burning flesh? He fled the bedroom, pursued by the sound of heated debate. He entered his own bathroom, and above his right eyebrow, a red mark about the size of a half-dollar was taking shape. He felt woozy. He applied some cold water to the welt with a washcloth.

"Jesus Christ Almighty," he said, trying to rub away the mark that had formed on his forehead.

The sounds of conversation continued at high volume in the next room.

CALVIN DID NOT need a doctor's opinion to conclude that the television set was dangerous and ought to be removed, but he was relieved to know that his burns were not very serious. "We used to see these fairly frequently some years ago," he was told by the young dermatologist who treated him at the Health Center. "It's a mild form of radiation poisoning associated with leaky color television. I thought they had recalled all those sets. Nothing to worry about, but if I were you, I'd take a look at my warranty and see if that set can be replaced."

Calvin did not bother looking for the warranty. Instead, he called a carpenter named Finch from Buildings and Grounds, who spent the better part of a day trying to match up the molding and paneling of Peter's cabinet with new construction. It wasn't a bad job under the circumstances, and Susan was pleased to see that where the Zenith had been, there were now ample shelves for books. Finch was pleased, too—he got the set, after Calvin had warned him fully of its dangers.

Calvin was *not* pleased. He hated enigmas, and this one still had not been solved to his satisfaction. He spent a few hours in the basement, examining the circuit breakers. Finally, he concluded that the problem was in the TV cable system, glad to attribute it to the mysteries embedded in the arcane realm of modern technology.

Calvin and Susan were unusually tender to each other over the next week, and especially solicitous of Peter. As for the child, he basked in the new confidence his parents were investing in him. His skateboard was restored—accompanied by a brand-new set of trucks and wheels. And Cal felt the old family bond recovering all its strength and firmness.

October was in the air, and a faint russet tinge was edging the leaves of the maples in back of the house. The roses were still in bloom, and the chrysanthemums this year were dazzling. It was Calvin's pleasure to admire the changing autumnal colors from his bathroom window each morning while he was washing. One morning, on an unusually bright and brilliant day, something odd occurred. Cal was in the midst of shaving. He had applied the cream to his face and was preparing to run the first strokes of his razor over his stubble when he noticed that the surface of the cabinet mirror was beginning to lose its luster. His features were fading, as if his face were being obscured by steam from the hot-water faucet. He rubbed the mirror with a washcloth. Slowly, his features began to reappear in cloudy outline in the cabinet mirror.

When he lifted his razor to continue shaving, however, he noted with a distinct jolt that he was not looking at his own features at all. The face in the mirror was that of a younger man, wearing a checked safari jacket and love beads, puffing on a long thin cigar. The image changed, and he was looking at a blond woman in a striped sweater, carefully coiffed and smiling broadly. Calvin thought he recognized her; it was Dinah Shore. Suddenly, the bathroom was filled with her cheerful voice, as she questioned the man about the work he did on a program called *Hollywood Squares.* Calvin watched just long enough for her to identify the man as Paul Lynde—"We are here to pay tribute to this marvelous human being who has contributed so much to this industry"—before he poked his head outside the bathroom to shout for Susan.

His wife was downstairs in the kitchen, fixing boiled eggs and coffee. Something in Calvin's tone frightened her and, ascending, she almost lost her footing on the stairs. When she joined him in the bathroom, the two of them, side by side, examined a mirrored medicine cabinet in which a frumpy, middle-aged housewife in an apron was testifying to the superior cleansing powers of fortified Ajax.

Susan screamed, raising the hairs along Calvin's bare arm. Backing out of the bathroom, she caught the heel of her slipper on a hooked rug and landed painfully on her hip and behind. By the time Calvin had helped her to her feet, the voices and the images had disappeared from the bathroom.

The couple sat together in the bedroom, Calvin's arms around his wife's trembling shoulders.

"A haunted house?" Susan whispered. "In the heart of a middle-class residential district?"

"More like a possessed television set," rejoined Calvin. "Maybe we ought to call in a repairman to exorcise it."

They started to giggle nervously.

"Or maybe," he added, "the Muse of Video is taking her revenge on you unbelievers. I knew it was dangerous to insult the new gods."

"Perhaps we're both hallucinating." said Susan, who had turned serious again. "Let's have another look."

But when they confronted the medicine-cabinet mirror again, their hands closely entwined, all they could see was their own frightened faces.

Peter returned from school later that afternoon to fix himself a peanut-butter sandwich and a glass of milk. He responded to his father's challenge from upstairs: "It's me, Dad. Where's Mom?"

"Shopping; she'll be back soon."

When he had consumed his afternoon snack, Peter climbed the stairs to find his father trying to remove the mirrored door from the medicine cabinet with a large Phillips screwdriver.

"Who do you think you are, Dad," he said wryly, "Mr. Fixit?"

Calvin smiled at him. "Just trying to replace this thing," he said, adding under his breath, "before it gives us any more surprises." The screwdriver slipped off the screw with a scraping noise.

"Brother," said Peter, turning his eyes heavenward, "when are they going to stop putting lethal instruments into the hands of breadwinners."

"Don't be wise, Peter," said Calvin. He took a few more turns with the screwdriver. "Say, do you know you slept with your mouth open last night?"

"No," said Peter, in the same laconic manner, "but if you'll hum a few bars, I'll try to sing the rest."

Calvin peered closely into his son's face. At that very moment, an odd rumbling noise began to vibrate through the stairwell. It was punctuated by the slamming of the front door.

"Hello, everybody, I'm home. Why don't you guys come down and help Mother with her groceries."

It was Susan returning from the market.

Calvin and Peter descended to help her. Cal imagined that his wife looked strangely made up, as if she had been dipped in a plastic fixative. The smile on her face was decidedly unnatural.

"What a crush," she said. "I thought I'd never get finished with the marketing. Well, come on, get off the starting line. Mother needs some help with her daily burdens."

"I don't think you need that much help, Mom," said Peter, taking a bag from her hand. "Everyone knows you can pretty well handle Dad by yourself."

The rumbling sounds filled the stairwell again. This time Calvin thought he recognized them. They sounded like scores of people laughing in a hollow room.

Susan was pulling a bottle out of one of the bags. "I'm a girl who likes things with character," she said. "Martini and Rossi . . . on the rocks."

"Wait, wait, be quiet for a moment," said Calvin. Peter and Susan smiled at him, blandly. "Don't you hear that? What's going on in this house?"

"Don't blame Desenex," said Peter.

"How do you like my new lipstick?" said Susan quickly, rolling her tongue around her lips sensually. "Lip Quencher . . . wet your whistle."

"I don't like it," Calvin replied. "I think you look extremely artificial."

Susan ignored him. She was pulling packages from her bag and placing them neatly on the counter.

"Oh, Calvin, I forgot," she said. "You've got to help me write some invitations to my high school reunion."

"Your what?"

"I was looking at my five-year calendar, and I noticed that I have a reunion coming up." She knelt down in front of him and threw her arms forward. "Give me a C, give me an L, give me an I-F-T-O-N . . . *Clifton, Clifton,* CLIFTON!"

"What are you *doing*?" said Calvin, appalled.

"That lady," said Peter wisely, "is going to get splinters in her tongue."

Susan pulled a large colored box from her bag and held it beside her face. "You know, darling," she said, "this all-temperature Cheer is tough on dirt but easy on your clothes. In hot water or cold, it makes things whiter than white. It doesn't matter how dirty Peter gets chasing the dog through mud puddles, this heavy-duty detergent will wash away the stains in all temperature settings."

"What dog?" asked Calvin.

"What mud puddles?" echoed Peter.

Susan began singing a few bars of a commercial.

"Stop this immediately, Susan," Calvin ordered.

"Weekends were made for Michelob," said Peter, burping on the last syllable.

The laughter on the stairwell was now joined by deafening bursts of applause.

The next morning, after he found Susan laughing at a rerun of *Welcome Back, Kotter,* which had materialized in her dressing-table mirror, Calvin decided to put the house up for sale.

Marian Mayer professed astonishment. The Warrens had occupied the house for barely two months and, as their agent, she felt obliged to warn them that it would be extremely difficult to find another buyer this late in the season, especially after the university term was well begun. "It's too big for us," Calvin explained. "I've made a mistake, that's all." A costly mistake, Mrs. Mayer thought—but then she could not be responsible for the fickleness of her clients. Secretly, she was not at all unhappy over the prospect of making two commissions on the same property in one business year.

Calvin decided to prepare for a quick move. He put his furniture into storage before he had even located another house. Hoping to expedite things, he kept only the beds and a few odd tables and chairs. If he had had his way, he would have taken up temporary quarters in a Howard Johnson's Motor Lodge.

What stopped him was Susan. She was in total disagreement with Calvin about the move and thought his decision precipitous. Her arguments were practical. Except for a small inheritance she had received following the death of her father, she and Cal lived almost entirely on his academic salary and her wages from the Child Study Center. She felt the family could not afford to drop five or ten thousand dollars in a panic sale. And besides, she was really growing to like this house, had grown comfortable with its eccentricities, and particularly adored the kitchen, whose conveniences she extolled in detail as if she had memorized all the appliance brochures.

Cal discussed the matter with her patiently but firmly. "I think we must accept the fact that we are in danger here, Susan, and the greatest danger may be that you don't recognize it. Surely you realize that we are changing, growing into something different?"

"How do you mean?" said Susan. "I don't feel any different. It's you who seems to have changed—all cranky and rigid."

"Really?" queried Calvin, raising his eyebrow. "Then how do you explain the fact that you can't perform a simple household task any more without talking about 'taste sensations' and 'real natural flavor'? And when you're not parroting commercials, you're acting like some fatuous housewife in a television sit-com. You, who used to hate television . . ."

"I don't know what you're talking about," said Susan, rubbing her hands with a moisturizing cream.

"No? All right, then, look at Peter. He used to be such a quiet, sensitive child. Now he's behaving like one of those smart brats on *The Partridge Family*. Why, it's even beginning to affect me. Every time you and Peter start your domestic wisecracks, I find myself cast against my will as one of those simpering fathers, the butt of everybody's jokes, on some nitwit family show."

"Well, dear," said Susan, patting him on the hand solicitously, "we must all be willing to accept our destiny."

"That's just what I mean," said Calvin impatiently. Can't you see you're doing it again?"

But Susan was too busy reading aloud the label on her hand cream to hear him.

That night Calvin lay awake, staring at the shadows on the ceiling, listening to Susan's heavy breathing begin to rasp into snores. It was peculiar living in a largely empty house, but he was glad he had insisted on it. Instead of providing him with a sense of security, the familiar objects of furniture had begun to seem ominous, as if possessed by an alien force. He was safer, he thought, with his family and the four walls; he would not feel entirely comfortable until they had abandoned this house altogether.

His leg shot forward in the bed, involuntarily, and a cramp seized his thigh. Had he been dozing? Susan had changed position, turning away from him on her side; the right strap of her nightgown had fallen to the elbow. Cal delicately withdrew the covers from his body so as not to disturb his sleeping wife, and trod barefoot into Peter's room. The boy was mumbling in his sleep. Calvin, curious, bent to listen, but the words were from some unknown, unconscious language. Peter whisked an invisible insect from his nose and murmured again. For the thousandth time since his son's birth, Calvin wondered at the extraordinary fragility of children and at the marvelous grace of their slumber.

Peter turned in bed, and at that very moment, Calvin felt a cold draft at his back. Turning toward the door, he saw shadows sweeping the hall, as if somebody had turned the lights on in the living room below. Calvin moved into the hall and listened intently. Nothing. The alarm system had been set for the evening; intruders could not possibly enter the house without setting off a buzzer and alerting the police. Still, without question, lights *were* emanating from the living room. He began to experience a rising fear.

Who had turned them on? Perhaps, he thought, he had unwittingly set the timer on the downstairs lamp, a device to

confuse burglars when the family was not at home. Then he
remembered that days ago he had sent that lamp to storage
with the rest of the furniture.

Nervously tightening the strings of his pajamas, Calvin
started down to investigate. He was in his bare feet, but padded carefully lest the carpeted stairs creak a warning of his
presence. Halfway down he could see that lights were flashing
in the living room, as if the walls were afire.

Calvin was not a courageous man, but when he sensed some
danger to his family, he was capable of valiant acts. Nevertheless, it took all the strength he possessed to enter the living
room.

He perceived giant figures swarming all over the room, over
the walls, the ceiling, and the floor.

Although most of these figures had human shape, they were
not human. What Calvin saw were two-dimensional images,
more than twice the size of life, gliding across the bare surfaces
of the room like fish in the deep caverns of the sea. The sight
made him dizzy, for the figures were confused by their numbers and the colors were dazzling. He forced himself to concentrate, but the images faded and changed as he watched. His
head was spinning, and his eyes were beginning to ache. Calvin focused his attention on one wall at a time, ignoring as best
he could the distractions from the other parts of the room. The
first thing he managed to identify was a burly man in a business
suit, his bald head gleaming under office lights, wagging his
thick finger at a dumpy, disheveled companion. With a start,
Calvin recognized Telly Savalas as Lieutenant Kojak. On the
opposite wall, flooding all the surfaces including the bay window, he noted six male and female human heads in square
cubicles, each outlines by flashing chaser lights and rapidly
changing numbers—then four laughing people at a long table,
holding up charts and pressing buzzers.

On the wall which held the fireplace, Calvin perceived a
football game in progress, the helmeted players moving into
contact at the scrimmage line like huge, padded, prehistoric

animals—and, unmistakably, Howard Cosell was now on the wall, sloe-eyed and slothlike, articulating silently into a hand-held microphone. Calvin turned in disgust and saw, on the opposite wall, the interior of a futuristic spaceship, its uniformed occupants staring at an oval screen on which a giant nova was bursting into fragments. His head pounding, his eyes blurring, his stomach beginning to heave, Calvin watched, on his living room ceiling, a police car giving dizzying chase to a black sedan up and down the hilly streets of San Francisco. Overcome with vertigo and nausea, Calvin staggered. His brain was reeling. A foul stench filled his nostrils. He felt himself turning in circles, as if being sucked into a vortex. One knee hit the floor with a painful crack. He let himself be pulled down by his weight and fell prone on the floor, snapping his eyes shut as a huge weather map, decorated with arrows, swirls, and temperature numbers, played over his body and the surface on which he lay.

Calvin screamed—but at that very moment, the sound of his voice was joined by a deafening clamor. All the images had begun to speak at once. The room filled with a Babel of screaming brakes, thunder, music stings, shouts, gongs, buzzers, cash-register bells, running feet, police sirens, gunshots, slamming doors, jingles, electronic beeps, crowd roars, grunts, crunching metal, news reports, jet screeches, thudding bodies, screams, fanfares, clattering trash can covers, explosions, animal cries, drumrolls, mangled machinery. And dominating the pandemonium, arching over and beyond it, as if in orchestration of the tumult, the sounds of canned laughter, of studio applause.

The cacophony, and Calvin's screams, had brought Susan and Peter down to the living room. When they arrived in the doorway, they saw Calvin, his legs splayed out grotesquely. He was lying on the floor. His body was smoking, and colored images were playing through the vapor. Watching the patterns, Peter was reminded of the blurring effect created by a speeding carousel, and enjoyed about three seconds of nostalgic fantasy before being brought up short by his mother's pealing laughter. He looked into her enameled face; he smiled into her bright, empty eyes. "You're in good hands with All-state," he said to his father's unmoving form, and stood in the doorway, secure in his mother's arms, dreaming of chasing a brown and white dog through a mud puddle in the rain.

AS FOR Gary Price, he was delighted at his unexpected good fortune. Newly appointed associate professor of biochemistry at Southern Connecticut State College, he had spent the first few months of the term with his wife and two children in the cramped spaces of graduate student housing. Having despaired of decent quarters for the year, he had just learned of an excellent house available for immediate occupancy at a surprisingly low figure. The sale was being made through Mrs. Mayer, since the previous owners were not present at the closing. The agent, who was holding their check in escrow, said they were temporarily out of town; but Gary heard rumors from one of his friends at Yale that they had simply dropped from sight and left no forwarding address.

The Price family was hardly inclined to question their good luck; they moved their belongings into the house the moment a van was available. Gary's wife, Martha, was entranced by the new appliances, but what particularly caught Gary's fancy was the brand-new Sony Trinitron color TV he found built into the wall of the master bedroom. With most of New Haven still on the aerial system, this handsome cable-connected set was a genuine luxury, and it added about fifteen new channels to the customary VHF and UHF frequencies.

Following a cookout in the backyard (probably the last of the season, since the nights were beginning to turn cold), the Prices went upstairs to test the TV reception. They found it splendid on all channels—so clear and vivid, in fact, that Gary and Martha decided, there and then, to rent the Home Box Office system, despite the additional monthly expense.

This night, however, the family watched the network programs and discovered, with considerable pleasure, a new pilot show on ABC. It was about a suburban family and it looked very promising indeed, because it dealt with subjects that a young academic family of modest means could identify with— the uproarious adventures of a professor of comparative litera- ture, his working wife, and their precocious ten-year-old son. The first installment of *The Warren Clan* (as the series was called) had to do with a rather astringent debate between the husband and wife over how much TV their son was permitted to watch. Reminded that their own children had exceeded their two-hour quota, Gary and Martha sent them off to bed, then returned to finish out the evening with some more TV. They watched the evening news on WNBC, followed by the weather report, and then stayed tuned to the *Tonight* show. Disappointed that Johnny Carson had still not returned from vacation, and mildly annoyed by his vacuous replacement, they turned off the set after the fourth commercial, pulled back the covers, and fell off instantly into a deep, dreamless sleep.

(1977)

PART V

PERSONAL
MOMENTS:
*Reflections and
Responses*

CONTENTS

ONE

Nancy Wickwire, Repertory Actress

ONE OF MY earliest, most vivid memories of Nancy Wickwire is of her long tapered fingers stroking the ears of an ass's head I was wearing. It was the summer of 1953 and Nancy and I had both joined the Group 20 Players, a newly professional summer repertory company at Wellesley's Theatre on the Green. Nancy had recently completed her training at the Old Vic School, after her years at Carnegie Tech, and now she was playing Titania in the first of two outdoor productions we were to do of *A Midsummer Night's Dream;* I had the privilege of playing Bottom. The Wellesley nights were perfect for that production—luxuriant, thick, and rich with stars—and I took such pleasure in watching Nancy float across the green, followed by her fairy train, I remember, that I almost missed my entrance.

She had a manner of walking and running that were peculiarly her own—long-limbed, loping, vaguely angular, and athletic—and when she spoke, of course, she could thrill you to the marrow with the rich music of her voice. Group 20 was virtually tailored for her talents, being one of the earliest of the post–World War II American classical repertory companies, and in that same summer she had the opportunity to play, besides Titania, a flirtatiously rustic Phoebe in *As You Like It,* a raucous Kate in *Taming of the Shrew,* and Julia in *The Rivals.* Fritz Weaver was her Faulkland in the Sheridan play (he was also her Petruchio), and the two of them managed to transform what is usually considered a rather trivial, sentimental subplot in *The Rivals* into a penetrating psychological study of love-testing and neurotic jealousy.

We used to await our cues behind the hedges of that outdoor theatre, and joke about such matters as the theatrical implications of her line in *Midsummer:* "Fairies, away/We shall chide downright if I longer stay." Was this a stage direction? Couldn't Titania just as well chide down left or center stage? It was behind those hedges, and over breakfast, lunch, and dinner, during that sleepy New England summer that I got to know the true value of Nancy Wickwire as a human being and as an artist. Her devotion to the theatre was absolute; she was the complete professional in every fiber of her being; and as sometimes happens, many of us in the company learned a great deal about the art of acting simply by watching her perform. Group 20 functioned only in the summer, so we rarely saw each other between productions—which is to say in the winter—but she never forgot her colleagues, and I myself was regularly to receive from her, every other month, a carton of those Dutch pretzels which she knew I loved, and which were manufactured only in her hometown in Pennsylvania. Oh, we had our reunions all right, usually around Christmas time when the whole Group 20 bunch—Sylvia Short, Fred Warriner, Michael Higgins, Fritz Weaver, Gerry Jedd, Jack Landau, Tucker Ashworth, Louis Edmonds, Eliot Silverstein, Jerry Kilty, Alison Ridley and Bob Evans, Laurinda Barrett, and later Ellis Rabb and Rosemary Harris, and her husband-to-be, Basil Langton—

would collect together, and try to find something to talk about other than our memories of those lovely summer productions.

Nancy's career after Group 20 was varied but spotty: She got a few parts on Broadway, usually playing the other woman; she performed, magnificently, in David Ross's revivals of Chekhov and Ibsen on 4th Street; she occasionally appeared in off-Broadway productions of Restoration and eighteenth-century comedies; but she enjoyed her longest runs on television soap operas. Those of us who had expected her to soar to the top of her profession like a comet could only shake our heads in disbelief at the indifference of the commercial theatre to this exceptional woman. But the time of the Broadway classical revival was over—the time of the Katharine Cornell *Antony and Cleopatra,* the Bergner *Duchess of Malfi,* the all-star *Three Sisters* —and with it was over the time of the great American leading lady in whose footsteps we had expected Nancy to follow. It seemed for a while that this particular gem—this beautifully shaped and finely polished jewel—was doomed to shine, unnoticed, on the ocean floor.

Still, Nancy never lost heart, nor did she lose that cheerful, positive, selfless devotion to the theatre which was her hallmark. I've only known one other actress with a similar commitment to the theatre as a whole, rather than to her own career, and that was Gerry Jedd, who also died at an unconscionably young age. People like Nancy and Gerry kept the idea of a serious classical theatre alive when most of the others were sinking into the plush security of instant fame or instant money on the TV and movie circuits, for both were totally committed, by nature and by training, to ensemble company work. For that reason, it wasn't until the rise of the resident theatre movement that Nancy began to come into her own as an actress (Gerry, alas, died before that movement was fully formed); and it was only in her last ten or twelve years that Nancy Wickwire was able to do the kind of work she was destined for. Seasons with the Guthrie Theatre, with the Yale Repertory Theatre, and with the American Conservatory Theatre followed in quick succession—all three, interestingly enough, based on rotating repertory, with its opportunity to show an actress transforming herself through a variety of different roles. And when she died, she was preparing to go on tour with the ACT in a repertory of classical plays.

At the Yale Repertory Theatre, Nancy was an example, as she was an example in every place she worked. Whether in large roles or small, whether playing Volumnia in *Coriolanus,* Irene in *When We Dead Awaken,* Rosaura in *Life Is a Dream,* Caesonia in *Caligula,* or the Major in *Happy End,* Nancy poured herself into preparation and performance with all the passion of someone embarking on a new career; never tired, never jaded, never coasting, her eyes perpetually glistening with the excitement of her next entrance. And it was at Yale, in her second season there, that she discovered a new personal happiness and vitality, through her relationship with Len Auclair, who sustained and supported her through her final illness and death.

This death has struck a gifted human being from our midst at the height of her happiness and achievement. How many shall we see like her again? Not a star, but something much, much more important, a theatre artist; not a darling of the feature pages, but a true collaborator without whom many fine productions would be the poorer, she leaves us feeling stunned with loss, knowing for a certainty that to be such an actress takes a whole heart and an ample soul. Those of us who have loved her and worked with her have all had our own commitment to the theatre strengthened, and we know in what direction we must go. For in saying goodbye to Nancy, we take leave of a living presence who has left not just her memory but her example behind; and though the theatre is the most transient of forms, a way of writing on water, a powerful example can be a permanent influence too, while a strong memory bestows a kind of immortality. As for me, I will always remember Titania, running across a green that is moist with night and saying, with a mischievous smile: "Fairies, away/We shall chide downright if I longer stay."

(1974)

TWO

Vineyard Passage

I SPENT my first summer on Martha's Vineyard three months
after I was married. During our second summer on the island,
my wife was pregnant. And by our third summer, following the
birth of our son, Daniel, we had taken up residence in the
house we had bought in Lambert's Cove. Place and family are
inextricable on this island, and we measure our years by the
passage of our summers.

I have lived in many cities, both in the United States and
abroad. I was born and raised in New York. I have endured the
last thirteen years in New Haven. But while it would be indul-
gent to speak of home when speaking of an island where we
have spent only one-sixth of each year for the last fifteen years,
nevertheless Martha's Vineyard has been the one geographical
constant in the hearts of a family that values emotional con-
stancy. My son's annual leaps in height are recorded in pencil
against the door jamb of our bedroom. A crude cross in black
ink on our living room wall signifies a ferocious fight between
my wife and me, six years ago, over the casting of a play. Down

the hill from the house in the woods, there still stand the remains of a platform built by my stepson as the floor of a tent in which he lived for one summer.

The examples suggest, however, that in the midst of this pastoral stability lies the inevitable pattern of change, and in my seasonal role of summer squire, traversing my land as an excuse to avoid my work, I often contemplate the alterations in nature and architecture that have accompanied our years on the Vineyard. The original A frame of our early-nineteenth-century house has now been joined by L's and H's, as we added new bedrooms, porches, and a dining room to accommodate our growing family. The willow we planted some distance away when we first purchased our house now droops over the roof of our new kitchen wing, raising fears that it might soon seek nourishment in the water pipes of our sink. The blue spruce we planted at the same time, which now blocks our entrance to the shed, is mature enough to convince us that our fears were correct, and it is green. The sassafras grove has multiplied like the weed it is, and the myrtle cover spreads over the land like a counterpane. In my walks, I frequently come upon some token of things past—a piece of toy lawn-mower with which my baby son used to imitate his father's labors, the rubber tire of a wheelbarrow, a remnant of the stone wall we moved some fifty feet north when we acquired another acre.

How curious our Vineyard life has been, then, as if we had spent here one long summer of fifteen years' duration, during which our children had grown, our bodies and faces had aged, our architecture had expanded, our vegetation had increased. A long summer of time in which, year after year, we had renewed strong relationships with friends that were suspended during the winter, found new fishing holes, decided not to risk lobster pots again, worked on the boat and failed to get the fanbelt tightened, lost the oil in the compass and failed to replace it, watched the seagrass accumulate on the hull and failed to scrape it off, lived with a radio that received but couldn't transmit, drank a little more, ate a little less, and finally reached the point where we could compare the summer's weather with a period of a decade past and agree with those who found it to be deteriorating.

What else had changed? The placement of the clams in Tashmoo pond—but not my pleasure in digging for them. Indeed, I have never fully understood why clamming in Tashmoo has constituted the single most delicious activity of my Vineyard summer, more even than the Round Robin tennis matches on the private courts of friends, or that first brisk exhilarating dip into the July waters of South Beach, or that outdoor shower on a sun-kissing day. Let me tell you about the clamming. I start out from the mooring in Vineyard harbor on my boat. I am past the Chop in ten minutes, at the mouth of Tashmoo channel in twenty. The engine is cut almost to idling, as the current pushes against the slight forward movement in the channel. I throw an anchor on Milton Gordon's beach, and with a yellow plastic bucket in hand, go to my secret place for clams. As I squat in the water at low tide, I can just see Milton's osprey feeding its young, the gulls wheeling over the Tashmoo beach, a solitary black duck in flight. I scratch through the sand and muck. A crab pinches my fingers and I draw away in pain. I am scrabbling the sand now with my ten fingers and my ten toes. A hard object responds to my touch —a nice-sized cherrystone. There is a tiny clam nearby it—I heave it further into the pond. I cut my finger on an open shell and suck the blood—a common hazard of clamming. In an hour, I have collected enough for spaghetti pesto, to be made from Lillian Hellman's excellent recipe, or for stuffed clams, or for an appetizer of clams on the half-shell for a party of eight. I have enough in my bucket, but a frenzy of greed has overtaken me. I can't stop clamming. Deciding to take only four more, I break my promise when I come upon five in one small area. I understand gambling now, and acquisition, and remember how hard it was to give up cigarettes. I am in the grip of a habit, and I love it. The return trip to Vineyard

Haven, the current behind me, planing on the waves, is the memory that I retain most vividly in the long winter to come.

The Vineyard, then, is my world of growth and stability, the capacity for change and the capacity for permanence. It represents the single season when work and pleasure, society and privacy conjoin in perfect harmony. T. S. Eliot's Lady measured out her life in coffee spoons. I, much luckier, have measured out my own in Vineyard summers. The sound of the West Chop foghorn, the cries of children in Seth's Pond, the barking of a faraway dog, the topping of trees in Mohu, my neighbor naked on his tractor tilling the soil of his meadow, the goofy pigeon-toed quail scurrying in a panic as we come up our dusty driveway, the mouse droppings that inevitably appear upon the stove when we leave the house for more than three days, the phallic mushrooms that bloom near my study after a night of hard rain—these and much, much more are the images of my passage, the tokens of my sojourn on this island of summer and of change.

(1978)

THREE

Styron's Choice

FOR A LARGE man, Bill Styron has remarkably small hands and feet; they are for him a source of physical pride. On this particular day in August of 1978 (it is growing to dusk on Martha's Vineyard), his hands stroke a bottle of Tuborg beer while his bare feet perch carelessly on a coffee table, thrust amid a number of magazines and books. Styron has heard the sound of a friend's voice, emerged from the small cabin-study where he has been secluded since late morning, and in that curious shambling gait of his, pushed through the screen door of the main house. The friend is invited to sit and talk, offered a cigar, and asked if he wants a drink. Styron is thirsty for conversation.

As this time of day, during this particular summer, Styron finds it difficult to resist the sound of human voices. Immersed in his labors, he has not used his own soft Virginia voice for a few hours, and so he spends some moments hawking and clearing his throat. Styron is stuck in a painful section of the new book. His ears detect distraction with the sensitivity of insect feelers. He has always written slowly, making his way through a novel laboriously, like a hermit crab negotiating a series of huge boulders. But *Sophie's Choice,* in the making for over ten years, has become something of a legend for the time it is taking to compose.

Some say the book doesn't exist, that Styron doesn't even write in his study, that he spends his days in there sleeping and scratching himself. He has taken to wearing his pajamas at odd hours, sometimes for three days at a time. They are soiled with coffee and juice stains. When he takes his regular late-morning walk to the Vineyard Haven post office, he throws on a pair of worn khaki trousers. This walk may be the only regularity in his life at present; he has not been absolutely fastidious in his shaving habits or toilet. His soft hair is tangled and his lazy eyes are developing a slight film. Other habits are being abandoned too. Styron owns a half-interest in a twenty-one-foot Wasque lobsterboat called *Diabolique;* it is moored right off his dock, but he hasn't used the thing more than once or twice since June. Never a passionate lover of sun and surf (nobody has ever seen him submerge his body fully in the cold Northern waters of the Vineyard), he has now begun to avoid the outdoors altogether, wandering from room to room, from house to study and back again, like a doomed soul.

Another odd change has come over the man. Normally the embodiment of Southern courtesy, eminently sociable and affable, he has turned a little irritable this year, noticeably curt in his manner. At one party, he drove up to the house of his host, took one look at the guests from his car, and turned the vehicle around and went home. Once, when Rose held a dinner party without clearing the guest list with her husband, Styron refused to join the table. He forgets invitations he has accepted, or accepts two invitations for the same night, or rejects invitations with no explanation or excuse. He has even quarreled with his beloved old friend, Lillian, over the ownership of some crabs he had deposited in her refrigerator.

Today, he is impatient with his wife, with his children, with his entire household. "Rose," he yells. "ROSE!!! Where's the goddamn ice? Just like her to run out of ice." Rose comes running in from the lawn, where she has set up an office table to work on her poetry, between making calls on behalf of Amnesty International. Calm and collected in her upper torso, accelerating like a piston from the waist down, she is the human embodiment of what the Supreme Court has called deliberate speed. "Darling," she says with a smile, her patience further maddening Bill, "It's in the ice maker. Did you look there?" "I didn't know we had a goddamn ice maker," Bill replies. "I know there's nothing in the freezer." "We've had one for two years," she answers. "Well, get some ice then," Bill says. "Bob needs a drink. And get me another beer."

He talks to women with the imperiousness of a nineteenth-century patriarch; yet, such is the sweetness of his bark, and the harmlessness of it, that even the most liberated seldom take offense. As for hospitality, he has no peer as a host when the mood is on him. Styron will spend hours in the kitchen on a steaming day, preparing his celebrated Virginia ham, dipped in a glaze of bourbon, or his delectable Southern crab cakes, and he will serve them personally to fifteen or twenty delighted guests, enjoying their pleasure in his culinary gifts as if he had no greater destiny than to feed the hungry. And this passionate hospitality extends to literature. For an American writer, he is surprisingly lacking in vanity or self-regard, almost excessively generous in his admiration for others. The campaign against *The Confessions of Nat Turner* by black and Communist critics hurt him deeply—more deeply than he wanted anyone to know—but it did not make him publicly defensive, nor did it sour him toward the profession of literature, not even toward those literary vultures who exulted in his distress. He preserves the extraordinary capacity, so unusual in this country, to separate the work from the personality, as he keeps his own personality poised so impersonally within his own fiction.

One way we knew how much he was suffering from the attacks on *Nat Turner* was the way it increased his fears about his health. Styron has always possessed more than a hint of hypochondria (his semiautobiographical play, *In the Clap Shack,* is about how a young Marine mistakes a simple case of trench mouth for a syphilis infection), but after the *Nat Turner* incident, his physical terrors mushroomed. He is now the reigning Talmudic scholar of *Merck's Manual,* with the capacity not only to identify every disease for which you can provide a symptom, but to expatiate on the etymology, treatment, prognosis, and entire history of the disease from its obscure beginnings. In conversation, he may begin to take his own pulse in the middle of a sentence, or palpate his chest, or explore his liver, or knead his belly. Whatever illness you can name he has already suffered in his imagination. A robust man with robust appetites, he is nonetheless in continual combat with his body, which he regards as a secret invidious traitor, poised always to strike him down. Only twice, to my knowledge, has his body ever threatened to confirm his suspicions of it. Once, when a doctor detected a shadow on his kidney and Styron underwent painful, anguished tests in Mass. General before it was determined he was free from malignancy. And once, when a single marijuana joint induced such ferocious hallucinations and paranoid delusions that he had to be hospitalized for a day.

This summer, Styron's hypochondria seems to have returned, after several years of remission. And with it, that curious irascibility, that uncharacteristic crankiness, upon which I have remarked. All of his friends are remarking on it, too, for it is beginning to affect all of his friends. Oh, Styron's nature has always been volatile, but previously, his fury was usually directed, righteously, against fools and knaves: the prison authorities who had mistreated a black inmate with literary gifts, in Danbury jail; the "creep" developer attempting to turn the land around Styron's beloved Tashmoo pond into one-acre lots with a marina; the "unspeakable" bureaucrats responsible for imprisoning Soviet dissidents; the perpetrators of the Vietnam war; the Connecticut officials who unjustly accused a Litchfield boy of killing his mother. But now his rage has turned inward, where it has been touching those who love him most.

How could we know he was giving birth to Auschwitz? How could we know that not only his protagonist, Sophie, but the very author of her torment had been forced into an agonizing choice—to base a fictional work on the most awesome event in human history, and to place that event within a personal narrative, with daring comic overtones, concerning his early experiences as a young unfulfilled writer and lover in New York? On this very summer day, perhaps, as he and his friend drink together in the living room of his Martha's Vineyard home, Styron has been wrestling on the bloody mat with the ghastly relationship between Sophie and Rudolf Höss, commandant of Auschwitz. He is nearing the completion of his painful masterpiece, and it is tearing him to pieces.

Unlike many writers, Styron tends to be reticent about his books until he completes them, but during the making of *Sophie's Choice,* he has been positively secretive. True, he published a long, deliciously funny episode in *Esquire* concerning an encounter between Stingo, the horny hero, and that classic cockteaser, Leslie Lapidus, but this gave no clue to the actual content of the book. Also true, he wrote a short Op Ed piece for the New York *Times* in which he spoke feelingly on behalf of the forgotten non-Jewish victims of Auschwitz, but this was remarkable only for enraging the more chauvinistic editors of Jewish magazines.

Nobody, neither Rose, nor the children, nor his closest friends, has been permitted more than fragmentary knowledge of the new book's true nature. For reasons of his own, Styron has determined to carry the burden of this concentration camp entirely on the portals of his own heart. The long years of research, followed by the longer years of composition, have been private years; and the agony of Sophie's choice and eventual fate at the hands of her demon lover, Nathan, were contemplated, experienced, and created by the author in solitude.

And this solitude was exacerbated by another agonizing choice of Styron's: To remain a writer of fiction in an age when fiction writing had been declared so problematical. The opinion makers had been telling us for years that the time of the classical novel was past, that henceforth the celebrated writers would be personal journalists and cultural sports. Writing on the moment and of the moment, pirouetting around the media in a ballet of ideology and fashion, the celebrities of our literary culture, we were told continually, had virtually routed the "old-fashioned" novel, and with it, the very concept of a literary tradition. Yet, here was William Styron still working slowly and carefully, in relative obscurity for more than a decade, watching his name disappear from the lists of leading American writers, on a major work of literature in the tradition of Tolstoi and Thomas Mann—a work that does not exclude the personal element, but rather measures its size against the magnitude of history.

A choice that constitutes a singular act of courage and devotion, for which American literature is richer both for the important book produced and for the example of its composition. A choice, too, of which the author is obviously conscious, for the book is permeated with his awareness that he may have embarked on a quixotic, risky, absurd, and ultimately fruitless venture. A choice, though, that may not have been volitional, for William Styron is a classical writer to the very soles of his feet.

Those feet are resting on top of the finished works, galley proofs, and magazine stories of his contemporaries, as he downs a third bottle of beer in the company of his friend and his wife. The house is beginning to fill with noises: Polly has returned from the stables, Alexandra from the beach, Tommy from his sailing race, and Susannah is expected that night from her theatre in New Hampshire. Rose wants to throw a benefit party on Sunday to support Isabelle Letelier's crusade to bring the killers of her husband to justice, but Styron is not at the moment certain he can face a gang of people. He'll let her know. His eyes wander out to Vineyard Sound where the ferry is just beginning its approach to the harbor. The ping of tennis balls can be heard from the Yacht Club courts next door. That lovely golden light—which you only see on Martha's Vineyard, and only in August toward dusk—has begun to drape itself on the lawn like a yellow blanket. Styron gets up and stretches himself. The book, he thinks, will be finished in four months. In time for Christmas and some weeks in the Caribbean— maybe a trip to Venezuela. A respite from those endless hours at his desk—a release, if only temporary, from those dreadful, lacerating choices.

(1979)

FOUR

=====

The Last
Graduation Speech:
Going, 1979

TODAY, ALL OF US here are engaged in a significant rite of passage, this ceremony being the formal, symbolic expression of an important journey away. Perhaps because we are so seldom given to ceremonial functions, we cherish the few that we have: christenings, confirmations, marriages, graduations. Graduation, alone of these, is both a sad and a happy occasion. I've always found it revealing that it is also called commencement—not just an ending, but a beginning. And that really is the most appropriate way to approach our present ceremony. You will be beginning professional careers in the theatre, having concluded three or more arduous years of preparation, and the farewells that will inevitably, sadly conclude our experiences together will soon be followed by the greetings you are to receive where new jobs await you—those of you who have jobs in this curiously unstable profession.

I feel a particular kinship with your class—and not just because I happen to be commencing with you. During the three years of our work together, some very important things came to fruition, along with the inevitable catastrophes, which have cemented bonds between us. In these three years, for example, the DFA's learned how to supplement their work as critics with their work as dramaturges, not just standing outside production and opinionating, but actually entering the process creatively and contributing to the final result. In these years, the designers produced some extremely powerful metaphors both for the Rep and the School, developing a commonality of approach, for all their individuality, which could be truly identified as a Yale style. The playwrights found a way to work more and more under laboratory conditions, bringing their plays to the class in various stages of development, thus bridging the gap between solitary creation and full production. The administrators, stage managers, and technical students began to assume more and more responsibility for the running of the School and the administration of the Rep. And the actors and directors completed the first three years of a new acting/ directing plan, a training where each year would be devoted to a particular theatrical style—as expressed in acting, voice, movement, singing, and script analysis—designed to serve as a building block for the next.

This was the period, too, when you helped us to solve the complicated problem of how to bring acting students into the Rep without interrupting their training, on the one hand, and, on the other, lowering the professional standards of the company. The solution was a graduated relationship with the Rep, starting with walk-ons in the first year, understudy assignments in the second along with occasional parts, and featured roles in the third. This graduating class of actors and directors were thrown onto the Rep stage in a 1976 production of *Julius Caesar* before they had even finished moving into their new apartments, before they had time to find new apartments. The effectiveness of this plan has been demonstrated not only in the quality of the Rep shows over the past three years, but, more importantly, in the quality of the acting students. I can say, without any qualification, that you are the most imaginative, committed, versatile, and well-trained group of actors that have ever come through the School—and I am speaking of you now both as individuals and as an ensemble.

It would be difficult for me to rehearse all the theatrical achievements in which this graduating class has participated over the past three years: the happy and joyous *As You Like It,* the hilarious *Sganarelle,* the daring and imaginative *Naropa,* the twin *Sea Gull*s of the first year and the one we finished recently, *Wings, The Wild Duck,* the workshop production of *Terra Nova, Jacques Brel, The Radio Hour.* You were involved in the first tour that the Rep ever made as a company where you helped us check out Cambridge and the Loeb before taking up residence at the Public Theatre. You helped us beat Long Wharf in softball for the fifth consecutive year. You established the first floating bourray game in the history of the Drama School. You accepted the good days and the bad with the same equanimity and good humor. And when it looked for a while as if the School was going to lose its professional thrust, you helped supply the pressure that resulted in the appointment of a professional dean.

You are, in short, a damn good lot of people and I am deeply proud of you; I couldn't ask for a better group of colleagues to depart with. And you have this added symbolic dimension in representing the fulfillment of everything Norma and I, and the faculty and staff, have been working toward at Yale. What you helped us to discover this year, after thirteen years of search, was a genuine artistic community—a family of artists who, regardless of their individual talents and differing ambitions, could share in the values of a place. We theatre people are often accused, sometimes correctly, of being more petty, more competitive, more malicious than ordinary mortals, but it's also true that when the chips are down, we are capable of more generosity and love. And when the chips were down, as they were a few times this year, you anted up a lot of warmhearted support. Mark Baker and Richie Grusin will, I hope, forgive me for my poker metaphor, but one of the things I

want to thank this graduating class for is teaching me that the
secret behind a unified theatrical community is not so much
shared ideals, as I always believed, but a common passion for
five-card draw and seven-card stud. I assure you that I will use
that late-discovered knowledge in the coming years.

So we are engaged together in a rite of passage that is much
more intimate and symbolic than any of us expected when we
first met. Therefore, I would like to exercise one of the rights
of a rite of passage—a privilege initiated by the late General
Eisenhower when, upon leaving his presidential office, he
warned the nation against the military-industrial complex—by
trying to identify a threat that I have gradually perceived. A
threat that affects our profession primarily, but also, in some
curious, ultimate way, the nation at large—a threat to the
imagination and to the creative spirit.

One thing I think I have learned here is that the ultimate
division between people is not a split between conservatives
and radicals, or Democrats and Republicans, or Protestants
and Catholics, or city-dwellers and farmers, or middle class
and working class, or black and white; it is rather a split between those who love the imagination and wish to serve it, and
those who hate and fear it. This may sound as if I am pitting
artists against the rest of the world, but I do not believe that
a love for the imagination is limited to those who work in the
arts; far from it, I know a number of people practicing theatre,
music, criticism, and literature whom I think of as chief among
its enemies. Where you stand in this adversary relationship is
determined not by what you do, but by what you feel, by the
nature and quality of your spirit. It is determined by how you
perceive the talents and capabilities of others, by whether you
are open to or threatened by the unfamiliar. And I'm not
speaking of a permanent division either. I know many people
who began by closing themselves off from the imaginative
experience possible to themselves and to others, and who
ended with a total reversal in their perceptions.

So it is possible to be a carpenter or an insurance agent and love the creative imagination, just as it is possible to be a university professor and hate it. Our former house manager, now the fire chief of New Haven, was a genuine innocent about the theatre when he first began working at the Rep; by the time he left to take up his present post, he knew more about play production than many of our students, and expressed his greatest enthusiasm for our more difficult, innovative work. By contrast, a number of Yale professors who teach the imaginative literature of past ages—Blake and Yeats, Dostoevsky and Shelley, Spenser and Machiavelli, Proust and Joyce—are often hostile to experimental theatre, preferring comedies and musicals, conventional revivals, bland commodities. I find it significant that the most alert, demanding audiences of the Rep have never been, as you might expect, the members of the English department, but rather the epidemiologists and pharmacologists and psychiatrists and internists who teach and study at the Medical School. There is a marked, surprising chasm between the humanist and the artist—two professionals you would expect to be linked by common bonds—and this chasm worries me as much about the future of American theatre as any other problem in our national life.

So the division I am trying to describe is not a matter of class or educational level or economic status or color or sex or profession, though someday I would like to understand why women and doctors, Chekhov's and Ibsen's favorite people, usually seem more humanly open to theatrical experience than other groups. No, it is a matter of psychic generosity, of spiritual expansiveness. Those who fear the imagination really are afraid of life in all its unkempt, untidy, unpredictable disorder. They resent what cannot be categorized and pigeonholed, that cannot be organized into established principles and theories. One of the great limitations of institutions—and these include drama schools, theatres, and universities—is that they tend to attract those who seek security and order, those who fear the unconditioned and unclassified. My most difficult task, in thirteen years as dean of this school, has been to prevent an imaginative enterprise from rigidifying into an uncreative set of rules and regulations. I tell you, the pressures to domesticate and channel the energies of art into a smooth-running operation are simply enormous—they are pressures that come from others, they are pressures that come from the self. They promise peace and serenity and tidiness, all manner of good social virtues, but they must be resisted, because they invariably alienate talent and banish imagination.

So beware the instruments of precision that you will meet in the years ahead, the walking calculators and human computers; they are enemies of the imagination and, therefore, your enemies too. You are bound to meet them often because you have chosen a profession which is not solitary and personal, but rather collective and collaborative, and in such a profession they serve an important function. But their function is valuable as long as it is subordinate, as long as it services art instead of ruling it. Such people tend to rise to the surface because they are willing to assume tasks that others find onerous; and that is why you must be willing to do those tasks yourselves, or else accept their power. We are often told that art must be political. In this sense only is that true. The politics of a collaborative art demands your involvement, both as humanistic administrators and engaged performers, lest you deliver your fate to those who might inhibit it.

I have heard of theatres which determine their schedules by sending questionnaires to their subscribers, inquiring after their favorite plays; beware those theatres, they will not serve you. I have heard of theatres which base their season on the kinds of plays most likely to find favor with the current fashions of public and private foundations; beware those theatres, they will not serve you. I have heard of a large, prestigious theatre which is considering the replacement of its present artistic director with a computer, designed to measure what kind of play schedule was successful with audiences in the past, and what combination of actors, directors, and designers might ensure its continued success; beware that theatre, it, too, will not serve you.

There are obviously sound reasons why such policies evolve, and in a time of economic crunch, you can be certain you will see more of them. These theatres are filled with practical people, who take satisfaction in their hardheaded fiscal procedures. But if the management of the institution with which you work does not love the imagination, first and foremost, if it prides itself on being a self-perpetuating machine, then you are better off working in a factory. During our first year at Yale, the acting faculty was considering dropping a gifted student because she had missed a number of classes; Stella Adler exclaimed in fury: "We're here to serve talent." It was odd to have to remind anyone of this, but we need continual reminders. Not only schools of theatre, but theatres themselves exist to serve talent, even when that talent is unruly, and right up to that point (which occasionally happens and which happened a lot in the late sixties) when the talent disrupts the creative operations of the group.

Why all this emphasis on the individual talent at the expense of the institution? Because the institution was originally founded for the sake of that talent. It is the fate of institutions to try to socialize individuals, just as it is the fate of successful revolutions to tame or destroy their revolutionaries. As a French philosopher has noted, *"Tout commence en mystique et finit en politique."* But the politics of an institution has no meaning unless it preserves its mystique, its animating idea. And in the arts, the mystique is central to divine creation.

But what about survival? What about *Subscribe Now?* What about all the important administrative functions necessary to the well-being of the enterprise? We must practice them, and work hard at them, but only for the sake of preserving the mystique. I believe that a theatre or school, indeed any artistic institution that stubbornly clings to its original purpose, will eventually prosper and triumph, just as I believe that there are forms of survival which make failure and defeat look honorable. Because even if the effort ends in failure and defeat, the process of struggle is ennobling, and stimulating to the imagination. Sophocles understood this, and so did Shakespeare and Ibsen, while Chekhov knew that the creative example, even if momentarily stamped out, would eventually seed itself and multiply. These playwrights are not only our material in the theatre, they are our guides to wisdom; we must be nourished by their example, and multiply.

Let me cite one more example, a man not normally associated with the theatre—Plato, the philosopher. Despite his apparent hostility to art (he wanted to exclude poets from his Republic), Plato was an artist himself—and not a bad dramatist either, to judge by his account of Socrates' trial and death. Plato understood that the ultimate reality was not to be found in material things or institutions, but rather in the Idea, the mystique. This Platonic Idea is hard for us to comprehend because it is a spiritual concept, as vaporous as thoughts; it is something independent of the physical life that gives the physical life its meaning. It is the spirit that transforms and animates, that pushes us forward, that yields no rest. The institution without an Idea is a dead institution, no matter how prosperous or popular it may be at the moment, for it is a body without a soul. And the institution without a soul will inevitably be an enemy of the imagination, a machine for ironing out those annoying wrinkles of talent and art.

For some years, dark and difficult years, we had an idea here at Yale, but it sometimes looked as if we had very little else. We were far from a popular theatre, we were failing to communicate our purpose to students or company, and we were getting a little shaky in our own convictions as a result. In one moment of despair, Norma turned to me and asked, "What are we doing it for?" I answered, "We're doing it for Plato." For thirteen years, we tried to do it for Plato, and it was not long before we discovered that Plato was not a phantom, that he was in a lot more people than we had ever dreamed—as he is conspicuously present in this graduating class today. Continue to do it for Plato, and the enemies of the imagination will begin to lose their power. Do it for Plato, and you will help to fulfill not only your own dream but that of all your fellow Platonists, including Norma, including me.

(1979)

FIVE

Norma . . .

NORMA DIED three weeks ago today, on a wet cold evening, the last in a sequence of chilling days that cut through our flesh like a saw. The next day, a Tuesday, the sun finally came out. The crocuses appeared, the lilac buds, the daffodils, the thrilling colors of the fruit blossoms, all the tokens of the spring she had been waiting for through those long awful winter months.

There is so much to regret about Norma's death, so much that was premature. One of the things I regret a lot is that she didn't live long enough to see the spring. Norma was a child of spring. In April, she gained extra vitality. Liberated from the indoors, she careened wildly around town in her red car and wandered randomly through the city streets, peering into shop windows. She loved the summer, too, but that was something different. Summer meant vacation, play, pure fun on the Vineyard with friends. Spring meant the luxury of growing things, and, particularly, of helping things grow.

Norma was a daughter of spring because, deep down, I think, she really loved the ripening buds more than the ripened flowers. I mean this many ways, but I also mean it literally; during our marriage, Norma grew into an accomplished gardener. She liked to load our house with plants and flowers, each with their own special demands for light and water and nutrients. Norma, knowing each of these demands intimately, devoted herself to those vegetable creatures with a passion that sometimes made me jealous. Our first trip to the Vineyard was often uncomfortable because of Norma's compulsion to cram the Jeep with every variety of plant and fern. And when we returned in the fall, Norma invariably eased the melancholy transition by pruning, watering, and feeding for hours those plants we had left behind.

On the Vineyard, where she started with a flower garden, and then added a garden of vegetables, she was a demon with a hose. I have home movies of her, watering away with hypnotic concentration, as if that hose were an extension of her capacity for nurture. Our faulty pump lost its prime many times as a result of this obsession of hers with growth, and at least once a week each summer, I would be down in the cellar, working to bring the pump up to pressure, while she waited impatiently, hose in hand.

I don't need to tell you of her passion for babies, another form of bud that Norma loved. My wife was what the Germans call *Kindernarr*—crazy for children—and after Danny and Phillip had both grown past the need for powdering and pampering, oiling and diapering, she often threatened to kidnap the latest born of our friends and acquaintances. Norma put continuous pressure on Phillip, only half-comically, to give her grandchildren—she didn't care whether they were legitimate. And her constant appeals to our friends to leave their newborn babies in her care gave Norma a reputation for selflessness which she promptly derided. She simply loved small things; she even loved the word "small." In the early days of our marriage, before Daniel was born, she used to cradle my nose on her shoulder and stroke it like an infant—obviously not a small object, but a temporary surrogate for a time.

And she nourished and watered her friendships. The crowds who have so generously come to pay her tribute, the hundreds and hundreds who have written to us about her, all testify to the way Norma threw herself into personal relationships. Until she died, I had only a vague idea of how many lives she had touched. Decorating Maggie Scarf's bathroom, sewing a pillow for Lillian Hellman, encouraging Margie Lang in her newly discovered talent for making jewelry, helping the Dworkins find a house on the Vineyard, arranging a birthday party for Barbara Hersey, going over the manuscript of Ron Steel's new study of Walter Lippmann, decorating a cake for Bill Styron which replicated his book jacket for *Nat Turner,* staying up late after performances to talk over personal problems with students and colleagues—these were just a few of the ways that Norma used to demonstrate her concern and her devotion for friends.

But I think the most concentrated expression of Norma's attraction to growing things, during the past thirteen years, was the way she helped to nurture talent. Besides being an actress, Norma was a teacher of acting. She studied under a teacher she admired hugely, Stella Adler; and, combining Stella's meticulous techniques and respect for the dignity of acting with her own devotion to Chekhov, eventually developed a training approach peculiarly her own. Her development of this approach was never a casual thing; it may very well have occupied most of her energies at Yale. Going through Norma's private papers in recent weeks, I discovered that her written legacy consists primarily of twelve or fourteen half-filled notebooks, covered in that peculiar scrawl of hers with notes about objectives and intentions in scenes, and notes about the special acting needs of each of her students. Like similar dedicated people, Norma had no personal secrets. She left no diaries, no notes to herself, no protests against the unfairness or meaninglessness of life. She was capable of wonderful, breezy, witty writing, as a scrap of an unfinished novel she wrote suggests, and before we married, she had collaborated on two plays and a movie. But she always preferred to work with people, rather than alone, and her insights, her leisure, some of her deepest worries were reserved for the training and development of acting students.

From Norma, the most important thing these students received was not so much a warm personal relationship, though they knew she was always ready for that, as a remorseless, unceasing demand on them—a demand to respect their profession, a demand to push forward in their own growth. Working with students in the classroom, in that extraordinary first-year acting class of hers, or on the stage, when they were ready to play parts at the Rep, Norma had no patience with green-room bitching and "kvetching"; and she was never more angry than when some older professional actor in the company failed to set an example for her students.

Her effort to set an example herself was more costly than she let anybody know, but in a profession without many dignified role models, it was essential for her to establish an atmosphere where acting could once again be considered an ennobling activity. One of the ways she showed respect for acting—one that did not come easy for her—was to make professional judgments on the talent and development of her students. If she felt she had made an error in her selection process, or that a particular actor, for one reason or another, was unlikely to fulfill himself in theatre, she knew it was her obligation—both to the student and the other members of the class—to make her opinions known to the acting department. These were the most painful decisions of her life because her students were her community, and she valued their love. But it was a measure of her gutsy nature that she occasionally forced herself to disturb that community, and risk that love, for the sake of a higher idea. The benefits of Norma's personal sacrifice to the theatre at large are apparent in the unusually high quality of Yale actors since she began teaching her class—I believe that her eye for talent, her training process, and her example were instrumental in their later success.

And Norma was equally demanding on herself. She loved to act onstage, but she also felt she *had* to act onstage in order to earn her right to teach; the example she required of others extended to her own career. To play parts at the Rep, and to teach classes at the School, as the wife of the dean, made her vulnerable to much petty-minded malice, which privately caused her much unhappiness. But there was ultimately no other choice for her, considering her conviction that it was a performer's duty to teach and a teacher's duty to perform. What she quickly managed to do was to become an exemplary repertory theatre actress, playing bits, walk-ons, and understudies for years before undertaking her first lead this season as Arkadina in *The Sea Gull.* In *Ghost Sonata,* last year, she played the ancient Fiancée. She had no lines, she was made up to look like a cadaver, and she was instructed by Andrei Serban to play the part as if she were looking into her own grave. She hated the part for the depressing effect it was having on her life, she berated me for making her play it, and she refused ever to be photographed in it. But she did it. When Constance Cummings had to leave for London in the middle of *Wings* in order to honor a prior commitment last spring, Norma spent weeks memorizing the whole of that heartbreaking, mindboggling, tongue-twisting role for the sake of two performances, the last of which will forever be etched in my mind for its shattering power and depth.

Norma worked night and day on her roles. She broke them down, she researched them, she marked the breaths, she analyzed the intentions, she recorded them on cassettes and played them back in the bathtub. When Norma was rehearsing, conversation at breakfast, dinner, and bedtime was exclusively about her part. Her fault as an actress may have been over-preparation; it sometimes blocked her instinct, her spontaneity, her flow. During rehearsals for *The Sea Gull,* we discovered the secret discovered during preparations for *Ivanov:* that the essence of acting was to show not the effort, but the *effort overcome.* What the Italians call *sprezzatura*—doing the difficult and making it look easy. To get up in front of an audience the way Norma was required to get up was, I think, a signal act of bravery.

But she loved it, nonetheless, and during the last two weeks of *The Sea Gull,* she had mastered that difficult role entirely, not just with her head and heart, but with her breath, her timing, her musculature. She had discovered the humor and breeziness in Arkadina, so close to her own good nature, and she was having fun. For all her gaiety and life, Norma was not a strong woman, physically; I know now that her vital spirit, of which everybody speaks, was too demanding for her fragile constitution. But despite her exhaustion, and breathlessness, and occasional depression, she was able to bring that last role—the culmination of all the things she had done at the Rep—to a really beautiful fulfillment. God, she was wonderful. And she went out with the style that never deserted her. She had played her favorite character in her favorite play; she had finished the run; she went to a glorious cast party the next day in Roxbury where she had a grand, grand time; and she died.

I hesitate to add this personal note, but I think it is important to an understanding of this woman. The last thing she helped in its growth was me, and through me, the Repertory Theatre we helped to create together. When I first met Norma, I was writing *The Theatre of Revolt;* on our second meeting, I brought her my first two chapters for her editorial advice and encouragement. Norma read every word of that book, in every draft, as she was later to read and advise me on every book, every speech, every article I was to write. Having no other way to express the extent of my indebtedness, I dedicated my first book to Norma, calling her after Dante's description of his beloved Beatrice: *La bella donna della mia mente,* the beautiful lady of my mind.

For almost twenty years, Norma remained the beautiful lady of my mind, helping me not only in my literary growth, but in my development as a human being. When she first met me, I was an overprotected, sheltered individual—a Jewish

Prince, she called me—self-regarding, self-absorbed. With her incorrigible street smarts, she taught me about human nature and human motive, including my own, and by means of her witty, not always gentle ridicule, she tried to strengthen my character, always on the alert for any trace of self-pity or self-aggrandizement. If those qualities are in this memorial, I apologize to Norma; it is the first piece of prose over which she has not cast her skeptical gaze. When we came to Yale together, and encountered our first political environment, Norma became the principal strategist and backbone of the operation. It was Norma who toughened me up during the difficult days of the sixties and beyond; it was Norma who refused to let us be defeated when the whole adventure seemed to have gone wrong. We shared the same hopes together, the same thoughts, sometimes even went to sleep and dreamed the same dreams. Fiercely loyal herself, she could not tolerate disloyalty in others; it was Norma who fought ferociously by my side to make this enterprise succeed. And finally, it was Norma who may have given me the strength to bear her loss.

The theatre we built at Yale, and the theatre we are building at Harvard, belong to Norma as much as to any of us. Her spirit is folded into its aesthetic, its productions, its resident company, many of whom she helped to train, and into that vast and gifted troupe of actors, directors, designers, playwrights, dramaturges, technicians, and administrators who represent the residual company on whose talents the American theatre will be drawing for years. Norma touched hundreds of lives, and each of those lives, I believe, now bears some stamp of her humanity, her devotion, her generosity, her loyalty, her bravery, her feistiness, her sense of style, her humor, her radiance, her beauty. The most fitting memorial for my Norma, then, is a living memorial, an organic one. It is her two marvelous children, her family, her army of loving friends. It is the theatre for which she fought and struggled, and all the people, in the theatre and out, whose lives she illuminated.

She was not permitted to join us in the theatre we are bringing to Cambridge, but she is there, in us and with us, effort overcome. As she will always be in me and with me, my lovely golden girl, the beautiful lady of my mind and heart.

(1979)

Index

About the Author

Artistic director of the American Repertory
Theatre and director of the Loeb Drama
Center at Harvard, ROBERT BRUSTEIN has
written drama criticism for the London
Observer and the New York *Times,* and is
currently drama critic for the *New Republic.*
He is the recipient of the George Jean
Nathan Award in drama criticism and the
George Polk Award in journalism.
Formerly dean of the Yale Drama School
and founder of the Yale Repertory
Theatre, he now lives with his son in
Cambridge, Massachusetts, where he is
also a professor of English at Harvard
University.

DATE DUE

GAYLORD			PRINTED IN U.S.A.